THANKONOMICS

The Revolutionary Paradigm Change for Value, Money and Appreciation

Andrew Robshaw

1ˢᵗ edition, 2021.

ISBN: 978-1-9993780-0-4 (print)

978-1-9993780-1-1 (e-book)

First-page font © Adobe

Contents

Dedication

"This book and concept are dedicated to the British National Health Service and all the committed medical workers from around the world, that have worked tirelessly to save us all, and yet under the current system are accounted for as an expense, not an asset"

"The art of observation consists in this, the seeing of great things in little things, the whole in the part, even the infinitesimal part."

– Thomas Hardy, one of Britain's
greatest novelists (1840-1928)

* *Please note that the opinions expressed in this book are mine and a mention of anyone or any work in no way means that they agree or disagree with (or are even aware of) my views.*

In addition, although much attention has been focused on ensuring that the facts and statements in this book are accurate and correct, any omission or errors are entirely mine.

Introduction

Five observations that
will change the 21st century

☆ ☆ ☆ ☆ ☆

The aim of this book is to show you why:

1. Our current business and economic system misses much of the value created.

2. Value is the motivator that makes us want to choose, repeat the selection of, and recommend a person or organisation's productive output. The total sum of this value should determine the size of the economy. However, much productive output currently lies outside current value measurement systems.

3. Money is a concept that offers the right to choose other people's productive output at just one moment in time (the point of sale). That right should be an equivalent measure of the actual appreciation of the

productive output. It should be a right given by society as a thank you.

4. We should all be remunerated for the total level of appreciation generated by our productive output.

5. Passion is the highest form of appreciation. Identifying what we are passionate about and ensuring that we work for organisations that enable us to express that passion is the new nirvana at the workplace.

This book will lead the way to a new business and economic paradigm by observing and empirically analysing some very common misconceptions that plague our current system. The resulting paradigm will not only solve many of the current system imbalances but will also lead to a fairer, more equitable and sustainable society for everyone. Going to the very heart of accounting and economic concepts will show how and why exactly are they precise but not the accurate processes we assume them to be.

Accounting has historically been the best estimation of the fundamental purpose of business value. It assesses value at the point of sale. This assessment is taken from the seller's perspective. Profit, price, and costs are all set by the seller, despite value assessed and determined by the buyer. That assessment is also constantly changing both during the production process and after the point of sale as the buyer compares his/her preconceptions to reality. The net result of the current accounting system is a very precise, but inaccurate assessment of value. It also takes time to collate and analyse accounting information. This situation was acceptable in the past, as we did not have the technology to enable an alternative. Now we do, and this book will explain why, and what needs to be done to take advantage of our newfound capabilities.

Economics is a social science based on models and perceptions that are the best guesses of the motivations behind human behaviour. However, scientific research has now clarified and proved the real drivers for our motivations. There is no longer any need to guess, model, or hypothesise. We now know exactly what our fundamental motivations and drivers are. We can use this newfound knowledge to rebuild the foundations of economics, so it becomes a fact-based science where we experiment, prove, and record our results.

We will see in this book that true value is in fact measurable. The current economic measurement of value is like the Indian parable of six blind men describing an elephant via touching various parts of it. The man touching the legs would say it's a tree trunk, the one touching the ears would say they are a piece of hard, flat leather, and the one touching the tusks would say they are hard, pointy teeth, etc. Each would be more or less accurate in their descriptions of parts of the elephant, but their respective perceptions would be too narrow. Economics needs to go back to the fundamentals of human motivation and rebuild from proven biological facts.

Metaphorically, economics, in its current state, is like the pre-fourteenth century, earth-centric view of the solar system. It took the scientific evidence of Copernicus to prove that the Sun (not the Earth) is the centre of the solar system. This book will set out to show how the current definition of economic utility, (satisfaction) and the assumption that it represents value, misses a vital element that prevents a consistent result across all scenarios, and that many economic assumptions are perceptions that overlook reality to justify the theory.

When the effects of the current accounting and economic systems are carried out to their fullest extent, they result in distorted and profound negative consequences (unnecessary poverty, the distortion of earnings, a failure to support all of society, and the encouragement of negative externalities such as concentration of wealth).

To start our analysis, we need to truly understand the facts and logic of our accounting and economic systems. We need to first understand their fundamental drivers. We need to understand what we are trying to achieve as individuals (and why), in order to understand how we act as a group, as a society, and collectively as a global economy.

It's like the need to understand the infinitesimally small nature of molecule particles via quantum mechanics so we can understand the immensity of the universe. By starting right at the 'sub-molecular' level of our accounting and economic systems, we can put our individual motivations, wants, and needs into a biological and scientific context. Economics then becomes a true science based on facts, not on models or theories. From these solid and proven facts, we can construct a true economy that takes the demands of society, the environment, and the planet into account.

We go through life following a set of assumptions created by our predecessors. We generally take it for granted that those assumptions are set in stone. Yet in the case of our economic and accounting systems, some of the most important and fundamental assumptions are misleading. Clearly defining and investigating some of these concepts and taking them to their logical conclusion will have profound and far-reaching implications for current business models, work, and society.

Numerical versus subjective value

Using empirical evidence, this book proposes that there are just two forms of value as far as the human brain is concerned: numerical (non-subjective) and subjective value. A numerical value is a statement of a fact, there is no room for human interpretation. It essentially represents the financial economy.

Subjective value, on the other hand, requires human assessment and represents what we call the 'real' productive economy. It is more complicated, but it can be succinctly defined as '*the excess over expectations*'. Subjective value, therefore, requires expectations. There is the potential to have an excess over expectation (the creation of value) with any kind of subjective decision. Every time we make a commercial or individual decision, we should have expectations of the outcome. To not do so would be a very risky decision-making approach (as without expectations, anything can happen). We want to avoid random and undesirable results. Value *is the amount of appreciation of the excess over expectations for ANY decision that has the possibility of improving our present position.*

This book highlights the fact that subjective value is actually an emotion created by the release of dopamine into the brain when making a decision that fulfils, or exceeds, our expectations. The greater the excess, the greater the release of dopamine, and the greater the motivation.

As you will see in Chapter 1, this observation is based on the scientific discovery that the excess over expectations results in a directly proportional release of dopamine into the Nucleus Accumbens (the main reward centre in the brain). When we buy an article or make a decision, if the decision exceeds our expectations, we have a strong desire to take, repeat or recommend (TRR) the action.

For example, whether we buy a pair of jeans or decide to go on holiday, if our expectations are fulfilled or exceeded, we will want to 'TRR' the experience. Making a decision is a highly subjective process; we set our own expectations, and, using these expectations, determine whether they have been exceeded (or not). In effect, we 'price' value through our level of appreciation.

The concept of subjective value also applies to our interactions with others, including at the workplace. If our interactions with people are suitable or exceed our expectations, we will want to interact with them again, or even recommend them to other people (TRR).

Fulfilling expectations can even exceed a person's 'true' expectations simply because of the variability of the norm. That's because we sometimes discount our expectations. We know from experience that 'the cheque is in the post' doesn't always mean that, and when it does arrive 'as expected' (or even within a few days), we are mildly surprised. We are much more likely to want to 'TRR' dealing with the person or organisation.

However, although we are beginning to widen our assessment of subjective value to include happiness, well-being, and social impact, this book proposes that we should be focusing on assessing appreciation. There are a whole range of reasons why we should be focused on assessing appreciation which will be explained in detail later in the book. Put simply, they can be summed up by the saying: "if you don't appreciate something, it has no value". The word 'appreciate' comes from the Latin 'ad pretium', to price. Value should therefore be measured or priced by appreciation; the value in value is appreciation.

Yet, despite the widespread existence of excesses over expectations, the current accounting method only assesses value as the commercial value, or price, at the point of sale. Yet there are many more decisions affecting the perceived value of productive output long before then (e.g., design, production, distribution, and marketing), as well as after the point of sale (e.g., product quality, duration, efficacy, and after-sales support).

In addition, many organisations and individuals don't even have a point of sale to assess their productive output. For example, non-government organisations (NGOs), charities, the civil service, not-for-profit organisations, teachers, doctors, nurses, the police force, the armed forces, council employees, stay-at-home carers, charity workers, etc. We know intuitively that vast quantities of value are created by all these organisations and individuals, yet there is little to no assessment or monetisation of this value by an accounting system.

As a result of this one-off assessment of subjective value, most of society's productive value goes unmeasured. For example, we have the capability to accurately measure value in the not-for-profit sector by putting its jobs on par with the commercial sector. If this were to happen, not-for-profit sector workers would no longer be seen principally as a cost but as an asset, and remunerated accordingly, just as 'frontline' sales, marketing, and management roles are.

If we were to measure and monetise all the unregistered value of productive output in society, the amount of recorded value in (and hence the size of) the real economy would increase dramatically. As long as the money supply is kept carefully in line with this 'new-found productivity', there should be no inflationary effect. These large increases in the size of the economy should effectively remove, or at least, greatly diminish, poverty as an issue. However, as of yet, we have not updated our current system of only focusing on 'commercial' value. We are missing out on the value creation in the rest of an organisation both before and after, the point of sale, as well as missing the value creation in organisations that don't have a point of sale.

Current accounting methods are inaccurate due to the innate characteristics of value. At best, price is an average of other people's perceptions. All types of subjective value are measured on the same neural scale. Before the technological age, it was impossible to monitor value fluctuation points. However, with today's computing power and the communication networks we have, it is entirely possible to accurately assess value fluctuations close to real-time.

As we will see in Chapter 2, economics assesses value as utility (satisfaction), a vague term that, they say, can't be measured that is the usefulness of the preference. However, the brain's reward centre receives no stimulation (dopamine) from the preference selected or getting the choice right, only for exceeding expectations.

Economics also misses much of value creation on a macro scale because the gross domestic product (GDP) of an economy represents only a small proportion of our productive output. It certainly takes no account of externalities such as the effects of production on the climate and planet.

When we look at the characteristics of value, they show that our accountancy system (and hence our assessment of the form and size of the economy) could be significantly more accurate than it is currently. The economy is supposed to be an assessment of the amount of value created and if most of that value is not being captured, something needs to be done.

A new paradigm and measurement system is required to fully assess our productive output throughout its production, acquisition, and disposal. This book will suggest a new paradigm along with how current data capture methods can be adapted to assess value that is accurate, real-time, and predictive. I will explain how to use these common and widespread methods for obtaining an accurate valuation of the productive output of not only an organisation as a whole but also at the individual, team, group and section levels so that investors and managers can accurately see the effect of their decisions almost in real-time.

This paradigm shift will result in people being paid based on the true value that they produce. It will represent a significant increase in income for most, and everyone will have the ability to improve the support that they get, the quality of their management, and the resources they have available. People should be happier, feel better at work and be much more productive.

The few that don't create much value, either because they are not happy with, or are simply not good at their job, can be gently re-directed to where they are more content to contribute. The new system should enable people to identify what they are good at (and passionate about) to facilitate career moves. Changing jobs will be perceived as a realignment rather than a rejection.

The new system will still be based on the evaluation of productive output (i.e., those aspects of our lives where we use our knowledge and capabilities for the purpose of assisting someone else that we might or might not know), just as our current work activity is evaluated by productive output. We go through school to obtain knowledge, to find out what we are good at and what we would like to do to contribute to society. Although elements of our social capacity, such as our sociability and sensitivity, will be assessed as being an important part of carrying out our work role, it needs to be emphasised at the outset that this proposed new system has no role in assessing our social value.

Chapter 1

The science behind value

Despite any belief to the contrary, we are a result of programming by natural selection. All life on Earth has been focused on ensuring its survival for nearly 3,500 million years, 'building' increasingly sophisticated DNA master programs. Evolution's 'ability to react' is dependent on the generation time (from 20 minutes in bacteria to 20 years in humans)[1], and exists due to DNA copying errors. These mutations supply a range of possible alternative solutions to changes or threats in the environment. The strongest, or best adapted, survive in Darwin's famous 'survival of the fittest' concept in evolutionary theory.

Another evolutionary method to react to changes is to create a 'conscious capacity'. This capacity enables the species to identify changes, adapt, and react much faster and more intelligently than via the random process of DNA transcription error and having to wait for the effects on the new generation. Conscious thought gives a tremendous advantage to the survival of a species.

The sensation of value is a genuine, conscious feeling in people. Our brain structure and chemical messengers, such as dopamine, affect our conscious control. Our DNA is, therefore, able to influence our behaviour. However, so much freedom is potentially dangerous if an individual is not totally focused on survival. So, our genetic programming 'guides' us by creating chemicals and sending electronic messages that can encourage us, whether consciously, or not, to act in a specific way. In effect, we are manipulated, trained, and coerced into necessary behaviours and actions, whether we like it or not. Our evolution is too valuable to be left to the quirky choices of individuals. We (and all species in general) are programmed, wired, and chemically stimulated to focus on genetic survival.

It should, therefore, be no surprise to discover that part of the programming and structure of the human brain encourages us to learn, to improve, to realise and to fulfil our individual capabilities to maximise the likelihood of our survival. Part of our reward system is a group of neural structures that create chemicals to form sensations such as wanting (where we are motivated to take action to obtain something), liking (where we might enjoy something but are not necessarily willing to take action to obtain it), pleasure, hunger, fear, anger, boredom and excitement. These sensations are created by hormones such as adrenaline, oxytocin, opioid peptides and testosterone, and neurotransmitters (dopamine and serotonin) in the brain or elsewhere in the body.

Inside our brain (and those in many other species) is a range of training systems to ensure that the conscious decisions we make are focused on improving our own (and our immediate society's) situation and survival. That doesn't necessarily mean that we will get our decisions right or that we won't make detrimental decisions, but the system is there, and it operates during every decision or interaction we make.

We cannot survive or succeed without the assistance of others, so we are genetically programmed to want to contribute to the success of others using our comparative advantage (talents and capabilities) to offer services or products for the good of society.

We are constantly reminded throughout our lives that we cannot succeed on our own. This reminder is provided by our emotions (loneliness, sadness, hunger, joy, happiness, etc.) from birth, during our upbringing and into adulthood. We are constantly requiring the assistance of others. To obtain that assistance, we are genetically and emotionally programmed (contrary to much political dogma) to contribute a significant proportion of our lives to the service of others.

There are many ways we contribute to the society we live in, through our family, friends, and social network, among others. Those avenues are outside the scope of this book (and they should remain so). The central focus of this book is what I define as our 'productive' output (the part of our output that is committed to the interests/needs of others who we may or may not know) where we expect to receive something that we appreciate/value for our contribution.

The parts of the brain involved in the motivation process

Rewards are a principal stimulant of motivation. They create positive emotions, and they incentivise a species to increase the frequency of the desired behaviour, and, hence, to continue to survive.[2,3] The principal region of the brain associated with this training system is called the 'reward pathway'. It has two sectors. Dopamine is produced in the ventral tegmental area (a very primitive part of the brain) and it is transmitted through the amygdala (which is used for emotions such fear, anger and sadness, as well as the control of aggression, our survival instincts and memory) and the hippocampus (which is important for learning and memory). The dopamine is released into the Nucleus Accumbens (NAcc) (the pleasure centre that creates desire or want), located in the striatum (which is used for motor and action planning, decision-making, motivation, reinforcement and reward perception).

This reward pathway is called the mesolimbic dopamine system and it is responsible for reward anticipation and learning sub-processes. When dopamine is released into the NAcc, it creates a pleasant sensation and a change of behaviour. (It is still being debated whether it is the dopamine itself that gives the pleasure sensation or whether its release causes a proportional release of another chemical such as an opioid peptide).[4,5]

Another reward pathway is the mesocortical dopamine system, which deals with encoding the relative value of the reward and goal-directed behaviour. It is the link between the medial prefrontal cortex (which is used for planning, complex decision-making, personality expression and moderating social behaviour), the anterior circulate cortex (used for understanding and emotion control) and the perirhinal cortex (used for object recognition and memory storage).

How the reward pathway operates

The brain rewards the individual for exceeding expectations (called the 'reward prediction error' in neuroscientific terms) with a proportional release of a motivating dose of dopamine[6,7,8], which is a common neural currency.[9,10] The brain does not actually reward the decision-maker for obtaining the reward, but for the amount, the result exceeds the expectations.[11,12,13,14] Research has also determined that there is no difference between the neurons stimulated by commercial or personal/social value.[15,16,17,18]

The amount of dopamine released is highly correlated to the magnitude of wanting (incentive salience) to repeat (and with humans, to recommend) the decision, which is determined by the excess over expectations.[19,20] The release of the dopamine (directly or indirectly), and its encoding into the NAcc, creates the sensation of enjoyment, success, and/or pleasure, which is appreciated (priced-valued) by the individual.[21,22,23,24] This sensation encourages a strong desire to repeat the action.[25,26] In other words, the more dopamine transmitted, the more the desire to repeat the exercise. The more expectations are exceeded, the greater the release of dopamine, and the greater the desire to want to repeat (*and recommend*) the action.

To prove just how powerful this reward pathway training system is, a rat had electrodes inserted in the part of the brain that produces dopamine when stimulated. These electrodes sent a stimulating pulse into the brain and a consequent release of dopamine every time the rat pressed a lever. Once the experiment started, the rat ceased all other activity, and incessantly and repeatedly pushed the lever, without eating or drinking, until it collapsed from exhaustion.[27]

This training feedback loop consists of a series of sub-processes such as creating expectations, associating the reward with the behaviour, working out a strategy to obtain the reward, encoding the relative value of the reward and updating the excess over the ever-changing expectations.[28,29] If the reward does not fulfil or exceed expectations, the individual will either not carry out, or quickly stop, the activity.

Applying the research findings to a practical and typical scenario, the brain uses reward pathways and their supporting structures when making a decision or interacting. Expectations are created about what is believed to be the optimum solution. if there is sufficient <u>confidence</u> that the decision or interaction will result in an improvement of the current situation, a decision is taken.

The brain then verifies if, and by how much, the expectations have been exceeded. If they have, a directly proportional amount of dopamine is transmitted to the NAcc.[30] This release of dopamine rewards the decision-maker for taking the action, encourages them to repeat it, and at least with humans, if it is believed that others that are important to the individual are currently unaware of the potential reward, they recommend the action.

The five critical characteristics of subjective value

As value is based on an individual's excess over expectation, it is:

1.   Highly subjective.

It differs between individuals. Everybody has a unique perception of the world, starting from our unique, 'never existed before' genetic code to an infinite variety of experiences and influences that affect our decisions and interactions throughout life.

2.   Transient.

Our feelings change constantly, which affects our

perception.

## 3.	Dynamic.

Our perception of value is also constantly changing due to new information, circumstances, and expectations. Hence our appreciation of the excess over expectations also changes constantly.

Pricing should also be dynamic to reflect this change in subjective value. At the moment, we only see the application of dynamic pricing in limited industries such as airlines and hotels. A new paradigm where technology enables dynamic pricing to be applied to any type of product or service makes sense from a valuation accuracy point of view. For example, the price of Coca-Cola should vary on a minute-by-minute basis depending on demand influences such as average consumption and the temperature outside. Discounts could be offered to customers via store loyalty cards. The technology exists to enable such a dynamic pricing system now and it could be used to optimise production, consumption, and pricing for both buyers and sellers.

## 4.	Ubiquitous (found everywhere).

We normally have expectations of every interaction we have and every decision we make. If we didn't, we would have no expectations of the consequences.

5.   **Bidirectional.**

Both parties have expectations in a customer/supplier transaction, so the value is exchanged in both directions.

Chapter 2

The problems with the economic measurement of value

There are two major problems with the current economic system of measuring value:

1. The concept of utility,

    and,

2. What is (and isn't) included in GDP.

The problems with measuring utility

Economic theory defines value as an immeasurable concept called utility[31] (which is roughly described as satisfaction). Utility is based on the three conceptual assumptions that don't reflect reality:

1. **Completeness** (i.e., we always have a preference among choices).

However, on many occasions, we are indifferent to a choice (for example, when it's of no interest to us).

In addition, as we have seen from Chapter 1, the brain does not reward the obtaining of a preference, only for it exceeding our expectations. This excess results in a directly proportional release of dopamine.

The level of dopamine is appreciated to a level that may range from satisfaction to delight. Whatever the level or effect, it is highly personal, variable, and transitory. Like accounting, economics is measuring a highly variable perception just once, and only in one specific area in the business context (sales). Yet both disciplines have been attempting to draw extensive conclusions on these extremely limited and narrow observations.

2. **Transience** (i.e., our decision-making is always logical).

In other words, if Choice A is better than B and B is better than C, then we would logically never choose C over A. Yet there are numerous examples of people making illogical decisions every day due to a desire for variety.

The economic concept of marginal utility holds that there will always be a progressive reduction in appreciation with the next unit (diminishing returns). However, the excess over expectations can vary greatly between individuals. It is not consistent.

For example, it can remain the same in people who gain comfort and security by repetition. Merely fulfilling expectations can also be sufficient to result in the same effect as an excess over expectations in some people, or even an excess, if they appreciate the same thing more (such as when someone explains the true meaning of a book or a piece of artwork to them). From a physiological perspective, there are clear indications of a common neural basis (learning theory) for reward prediction error and marginal utility (economic decision theory).[32]

3. **Non-Satiation** (i.e., we always want more).

However, there are plenty of situations where we don't want more. For example, when we have had enough, or too much, of the same thing. Marginal utility is always positive according to economic theory. Yet we can easily have more than we want (for example, too much food or drink can make us feel sick). We also can get tired of buying the same shoes or making the same decision (or loathe making the decision in the first place).

In addition, our constant need to fulfil the excess over expectations with just about anything, means people get satiated (or more probably bored) with the same thing.

These three assumptions of economics are used to predict our behaviour. Yet they are not representative of what actually happens in our daily lives.

Philosopher and economist John Broome made the

following observation on the concept of utility: "There are lots of conceptions of utility and since these differ radically, there is little point in collecting them together if utility were not already damagingly ambiguous."[33] He goes on to define utility as, "that which represents preferences".

The focus of economics on utility and that it represents preferences rather than expectations, is a subtle, but very important, point. If the brain was to reward preferences, the individual would be motivated to take the same decision every time. There would be no desire or incentive to improve or try something new. There would also be no innovation or productivity improvement.

However, as mentioned before, research shows that the brain does not actually reward the decision-maker for the right decision, but for exceeding expectations. The consequence of the difference is that an individual motivated by exceeding their expectations is going to be driven to try new products/services/solutions. It also explains the law of diminishing returns more clearly than utility does.

Expectations constantly rise. 'Today's innovation becomes tomorrow's norm.' There is a constant need to innovate to gain the same level of satisfaction. From a learning point of view, the excess over expectations (reward prediction error) encourages the decision-maker to try new methods and avoid stagnation. The sensation of value is a fundamental motivator for making decisions that have the potential to improve our situation. The strength or appreciation of that feeling determines our willingness to take, repeat, or recommend (TRR) decisions.

In reality, we are rewarded by exceeding our expectations. We also have an innate tendency to get bored with, or take for granted, the current situation. We are incentivised and rewarded for trying something new. That's why we are always looking for something innovative and improved to retain our interest, the theory behind why mobile phones are regularly released, with ever-increasing capabilities.

Economic utility can be ranked, but not quantified. However, excess over expectations can be ranked and quantified using an assessment of the appreciation of the excess. For example, a 5-star Likert system. This would be a crucial step forward in economic theory, and I'll explain how this can be done in Chapter 8.

The problems with measuring GDP

The economy is supposed to be a representative measure of our society's productive output. It is currently summarised as GDP, and it is measured from two perspectives that are supposed to give identical results.

1. Expenditure GDP = C + G + I + NX
   C = Consumption (willingness of consumers to spend)
   G = Government expenditure and investment
   I = Private investment in business activities

NX = Net exports (value of exports less imports).

However, this system makes no measure of the value of the output of those either not paid, or not paid in proportion to their true value. For example, what is the real value of the wisdom of a retired individual, the doctor who saves lives every day, or the police force that creates the necessary security for people to enjoy peaceful lives? There is also no assessment of the excess over expectations.

Expenditure GDP is the crude assessment (at just one point in time) of a fluid, multi-dimensional, process. This process occurs at every one of the interactions and decisions we all take while creating productive output, whether it be within a commercial enterprise, a not-for-profit organisation or at home.

Even within, and around a commercial enterprise, there are vast changes in value creation that go unrecorded; reputation, credibility, belief, confidence, trust, recognition, motivation, culture, focus, determination, commitment, expertise, knowledge, coordination, and support, to name just a few. Yet, the current accounting and economic system ignores, or makes a very limited assessment, of that value. The same can be said about the enormous amounts of value created within and around the not-for-profit sector and elsewhere.

1. Production GDP = COE + I + R + P + C + T + D + NFI

COE = Compensation of employees

I = Interest income

R = Rents

P = Proprietor's income

C = Corporate profits

T = Indirect business taxes

D = Depreciation

NFI = Net factor income.

As you can see from the above formula, again, there is no assessment of excess over expectations within or around organisations or individuals.

In economics, the principal assumption is that we must borrow before creating value. Yet, in the real economy, we have to give or create something before we can receive. In our everyday life, we cannot buy unless we have produced; there is no <u>wealth</u>, happiness, or well-being without creating, giving, or receiving appreciation first.

Chapter 3

The problems with the accounting measurement of value (and a new appreciation paradigm)

There are four major problems with the current accounting system of measuring value, that is, it is:

1. Inaccurate,

2. Delayed,

3. Retrospective,

   and

4. Ignoring most productive output.

Accounting measures a totally subjective, highly variable, perception of value, at just one point in time. Any accounting assessment of value (although precise) will quickly become inaccurate (if it ever was accurate) because it will be out of date almost immediately. It also misses the innumerable changes in value during production and distribution.

It takes days, months, or even years, to get accounting reports out, so the reporting is long after the event. In addition, the accounts only give an indication of what has happened in the past and very little indication of the future. Running a business or trying to invest in a company based on today's accounting system is like trying to drive a car through the rear-view mirror, with only a loose connection between the steering wheel and the tyres. We wouldn't dare do that with a car, but we are quite happy to run our companies and economy on such a crude system!

Further, there are many people and organisations that create vast amounts of value (such as teachers, doctors, nurses, home-carers, policemen, soldiers, and charities, but because their value production is not measured despite increasing attempts to do so), their contributions are not valued financially nor included in the economy.

The current accounting system can be summed up using the simple formula that is taken from seller's point of view:

$$Price = Profit + Costs$$
$$P = P + C.$$

However, the perception of value comes from the buyer, not the seller. Price is a 'best guess' of someone else's point of view. The system is also missing much creation of value by just assessing value at the point of sale.

We need a new, accurate system to measure all value and its fluctuations in real time. We talk about happiness, well-being, and engagement, but they all miss the roots/cause/foundation of value: appreciation.

- If we don't feel appreciated, we don't feel happy.

- If we don't feel appreciated, there is no well-being.

- If we don't feel appreciated, we certainly don't feel engaged!

What needs to be assessed is the level of appreciation created by an interaction/transaction. In just about any interaction/transaction decision, there is an expectation of an outcome and therefore the possibility of creating value. This can be summarised by an equally simple formula to $P = P + C$:

$$\text{Appreciation} = \text{Expectations} + \text{Value (Excess Over Expectations).}$$

$$A = E + V$$

$$\text{or}$$

$$A = E + {}^{e}E^{©}$$

It's important to note that, for any value (excess over expectations) to be created, expectations in the interaction/transaction have to be both met, and exceeded. For example, it doesn't matter how well a pair of jeans suit you when you try them on in a shop if there is only one 'leg'. There is no value in the jeans because them having two 'legs' is part of our preconceived product expectations.

Appreciation (value) is equivalent to the price: the amount of choice, resources, or facilities to carry out choices (e.g., time, money and expertise) that the buyer is willing to concede or commit to make the purchase or have the interaction. This value is supposed to be represented by money. Money has always been perceived as a measure of value. But, as a result of clarifying value as an excess over expectations *plus* expectations (i.e., as appreciation), money should represent the total appreciation created by the productive output of a person or organisation. in the new paradigm being proposed in this book, money moves from a one-off assessment at the point of sale to a multi-point, continuous, ubiquitous assessment of appreciation of the person or organisation. Money should equal appreciation. Appreciation should therefore be the basis of money. How do you measure the level of appreciation? We already do a lot of it by asking people to evaluate the products or services they receive.

Our businesses and other organisations should not be measured on the amount of money they make (as they currently are), but on the levels of appreciation, they generate. Buyers, suppliers, and employees should be questioned about their decision-making motivations to identify the levels of appreciation they have for those that work with them, be they other employees, suppliers or customers. Much of this information is already captured by peer-to-peer and other kinds of recognition software, it's just not considered or analysed as a value of productive output yet.

It's important to understand that there is a fundamental belief (exacerbated by the media) that people are self-interested and that when given power, they will abuse that trust. Yet the reality just doesn't reflect that belief. While there are always exceptions, people aren't generally self-interested, they want to be valued by society. For example, during the COVID-19 pandemic, the media focused on those that disobeyed the rules. Yet, the vast majority of people stayed at home and did their best to avoid catching the disease or infecting other people.

Appreciation in the workplace

According to an Investors in People survey, one in three of us are unhappy in our current role, and nearly half are looking to move on.[34] Lack of recognition is one of the major reasons for leaving a job. It's important to understand the difference between recognition and appreciation. Recognition is acknowledging work/effort carried out.[35]

Appreciation, on the other hand, involves acknowledging the person. In the words of Chapman and White in their famous book, *The 5 Languages of Appreciation in the Workplace*: "*While recognition focuses on what the person does, appreciation focuses on who the person is.*" They surveyed over 165 000 employees to find out their preferred means of receiving workplace appreciation. Receiving a genuine remark of appreciation was by far the most popular (45%), while only 6% preferred receiving a gift as appreciation. However, most organisational recognition programs focus on providing tangible gifts as their means of appreciating employees.

Employee engagement has been found to be three times more strongly related to intrinsic motivators than extrinsic rewards.[36] In addition, intrinsic motivation is a stronger predictor of job performance than extrinsic rewards.[37]

Chapter 4

Using appreciation as the method of pricing value

Both in its origin and our everyday vocabulary, the meaning of the word 'appreciate' is 'to set a price'. When we set a price, we evaluate. We put a price on the emotion of valuing something or somebody.

In its original Latin form, the expression was 'ad pretium' ('to price'). The word 'appreciate' first appeared in print between 1645 and 1655 to mean evaluating, valuing, identifying, recognising and highlighting the significance of something or somebody. Both the original and historic use of the word shows its purpose. The contemporary definition of appreciate is to know and accept the value of something.

Appreciation is the price assessment of value

Appreciation is essential for decision-making. It is also fundamental in the resolution of people's needs and wants. Our appreciation assessment concept is best encapsulated by the saying, "If we don't appreciate something, it has no value." Here are some example statements that demonstrate this principle:

- I appreciate/I value what you are saying/doing; your knowledge/experience/expertise.

- The value is in the appreciation.

- I don't feel appreciated, I don't feel valued.

- When I don't feel appreciated (or I feel I am taken for granted), I stop.

- I appreciate what you say, I value your opinion.

- You're a valued member of our community, we appreciate what you have done for us.

- An asset appreciates in value because more people want (appreciate) it.

As highlighted in Chapter 1, the same part of the brain is stimulated by value in the same manner, no matter whether it is commercial, personal, or social value. This appreciation of value occurs when our expectations are fulfilled and exceeded.

When something doesn't exceed our expectations, we do not appreciate/value it, and we tend not to want it.

Appreciation is based on excess over expectations (value). Anytime we are creating any form of appreciation and our attitudes are fundamentally positive, we are creating value. This notion ties in with much of the research carried out for the French positive economy initiative.[38] Examples of appreciation include giving/assigning/pricing value via recognition (public appreciation), gratitude, approving, liking, praising, admiring, respecting, acknowledging, perceiving, and comprehending.

Applying this appreciation concept to commerce and all other elements of our productive outputs and associated relationships, it becomes clear that the current business model based on accounting and economics misses the capture of much value. People need to be questioned on what they expect about their decisions in order to understand what they appreciate and therefore value.

On the other hand, any time we are creating any form of depreciation, our attitudes are fundamentally negative, destroying value. Examples of depreciation include disregarding, disapproval, disdain, neglect, criticism, disappointment, disillusionment, misunderstanding, and being ungrateful.

We act in the same manner (take, repeat and/or recommend) when receiving value as we do when we feel appreciated. Receiving appreciation includes receiving the excess over our expectations plus our expectations. It makes us feel valued. We like receiving appreciation. In fact, it is a fundamental need. We are motivated when we feel appreciated or valued. However, if we are not appreciated or valued, we are not motivated.

Motivation at work

Research shows that a major motivator at work is to feel appreciated or valued. There is a 10-20% difference in revenue and productivity in people that agree with the following statement: "In the last seven days, I have received recognition or praise for doing good work".[39]

Conversely, the lack of appreciation or lack of feeling valued is a major reason for leaving employment. Employees who report that they're not adequately recognised recognized at work are three times more likely to say they'll quit in the next year.[40,41,42,43,44,45,,46,47,48] In short, people's attitude at work is a major influence on either value creation or destruction.

A further survey done found that 64% of Americans leave their jobs because they don't feel appreciated.[49] Any lack of appreciation demotivates and destroys the productivity, as well as the innovation and creativity of the individual. Generally, the most important person to appreciate or assess the value of what we produce at work is our line manager; a problem with this relationship usually means stress and a desire to leave a job.[50] The trouble with this is that most people get promoted because they are good at their job, not because they are good managers of people. The same study found that companies fail to choose the candidate with the right talent up to 82% of the time.[51] Yet another study found that managers wished they had more training before becoming managers.[52]

We know that when we receive praise and recognition, we get a burst of dopamine (something that makes us want to repeat and perhaps recommend the action). When we feel understood, our reward mechanism is also stimulated.[53]

Appreciation is all-inclusive. It covers many of the principal motivators such as recognition, gratitude, admiration, praise, understanding, respect, approval, and support. An employee works for and is motivated by the appreciation received from work colleagues, managers, suppliers, customers, and any other people they interact with through the execution of their work.[54] Organisational cultures should be based on appreciation in all its forms as it encourages decision-making and the creation of value.

Chapter 5

How we appreciate

If you really want to appreciate the value in something, imagine losing it, breaking it, or throwing it away! It's only when we can't have something anymore that we fully appreciate it, whether it is a picture, a pair of shoes, or even a relationship.

That's why a good negotiator plays the part of a reluctant seller: "I really wasn't really going to sell this item because it's so precious to me, how much would you be willing to pay for it?" They might sell using a 'hot cakes approach' ("Buy now, because they will have all sold out shortly!"), or a time-limited access ("The offer is only available until midnight tonight"). The thought of losing the opportunity to buy something we value makes us speed up our decision-making process and can push us toward making a decision that we normally wouldn't have taken.

The importance of appreciating detail

True appreciation comes from looking at the detail and the effort that has gone into making a product or providing a service. To fully appreciate something, we must go beyond the superficial, and that's a discipline we have to work on. Appreciation is a form of recognition, for example, the more details we find from the bouquet of smells coming from a glass of wine, the more we can appreciate it. People spend years learning to discern subtle wine aromas. They can appreciate aspects that the untrained nose will miss. Similarly, we must also take time to explore the capabilities of modern smartphones in order to fully appreciate their benefits.

Noticing the detail allows us to find more excess over our expectations. It increases our valuation of a product or service. That's why taking things for granted is so destructive; it destroys value. Treating products as if they are all the same ignores any of its unique details. Similarly, treating someone or their output without appreciating the finer details, is destroying value. Appreciation is such a fundamental motivator; people do not want to interact with people who don't appreciate their efforts.

A survey in the US found that among employees who feel valued, just one in five (21 percent) said **they intend to look for a new job in the next year** (vs. 50 percent of those who said that they don't feel valued).[55] A variety of factors were linked to those feeling undervalued at work, including:

1. Having fewer opportunities for involvement in decision-making (24 percent vs. 84 percent for those employees who feel undervalued, a 60% difference).

2. Being less satisfied with the potential for growth and advancement (9 percent vs. 70 percent, a 61% difference).

3. Having fewer opportunities to use flexible work arrangements (20 percent vs. 59 percent, a 39% difference).

4. Being less likely to say they are receiving adequate monetary compensation (18 percent vs. 69 percent, a 51% difference).

5. Not receiving any non-monetary rewards (16 percent vs. 65 percent, a 49% difference).

Increasing our value through our self-esteem

Looking at the way we treat ourselves, we can adjust our value output via appreciating ourselves and increasing our self-esteem. How easy it is to be critical of ourselves or to belittle our successes and capabilities. Yet, being positive and constructive about ourselves can do wonders for our value output. This self-appreciation is crucial to our own value perception and capabilities. For example, our confidence and self-esteem can make or break our ability to perform in an interview, a meeting, or a presentation. It can also determine our value perception by others.

It can also be useful for lateral thinking to solve a problem. Lateral thinking requires 'thinking outside the box'. In order to do that, we have to shut our conscious mind down (which is not easy). This part of our mind is disciplined and organised. It's also very dominant and demanding and, hence, is not very good at making the obscure connections necessary to come up with 'out of the box' solutions. Our subconscious mind needs to be at the forefront for lateral thinking. Unlike the conscious mind, the unconscious system of our brain is shy, disorganised, erratic, and illogical. It is easily intimidated by the conscious part of our brain and condescendingly treated as mad.

If we or someone else doesn't appreciate the output from our subconscious mind (for example by criticising us or being condescending), our flow of thoughts dries up or even stops almost immediately. Yet if we respect our output as an important, constructive, and crucial stage of problem-solving, our subconscious mind continues rolling out ideas and making connections to help us solve the problem. The importance of shutting down our conscious mind is shown by the fact that our best ideas often come about when our conscious mind is not really operating, such as when we are taking a shower when we wake up at 3 o'clock in the morning, or when we are out jogging.

We benefit from giving as well as receiving appreciation

The more decisions we take that exceed our expectations creates more value. Showing appreciation for someone else's output also creates motivation for them to take, repeat or recommend. The value is in the appreciation. We clap, cheer, encourage (show our appreciation to motivate people to keep doing an activity). What's more, we also benefit from appreciating their success. We feel as though we're part of it. For example, when our national team wins a competition, we feel very patriotic because we value appreciating others.

Consider the reverse situation when we are jealous, derogatory, condescending, or ridiculing. The focus of our attitude will want to stay away from us. This is why positive thinking is so important. It is essentially appreciating everything we have and do. Everybody wants to be near to or associated with a person that sees the glass half full rather than half empty. We are all constantly seeking appreciation.

Chapter 6

The highest and lowest forms of appreciation (passion and fear)

If we are not appreciated, we don't feel valued. The highest form of appreciation in life is love. At the workplace, this translates to passion. At the workplace when someone is passionate about their work, they are the most intrinsically (internally) motivated, productive, and innovative. They create the most value (excess over expectations). They are not there for the money; they just love their job. The excess potential is nearly infinite. It's the same as when someone is passionate about a purchase. They love what they are buying.

Passionate people at the workplace are 100% intrinsically motivated. They are far more productive than someone who is just 'engaged' with their work. Engaged workers tend to be motivated by extrinsic (external) factors. Because these factors are imposed from the outside, they can quickly slacken off when the external factor is removed.

If we are not appreciated, we are unlikely to feel engaged. Happiness also comes from appreciation. You are unlikely to feel happy if you are not appreciated. Well-being (another 'in vogue' measurement) also comes from appreciation (whether it be self-appreciation or receiving appreciation from others).

Passion: the new 'nirvana', a state beyond engagement

Every company should be aiming to recruit the most passionate employees. A passionate/inspired employee is up to 125% (or 2.25 times) more productive than a 'normal' employee.[56] Research indicates that only 15% of employees are highly engaged at their workplace.[57] If the proportion of people that are passionate about their work is doubled to 30%, the additional size of the economy will be sufficient to pay for the entire UK education budget.

Passion at work is, as mentioned before, the new 'nirvana'. We should all be trying to find this highest level of being when at work, to the point that rather than calling it 'work', we call it 'fun'. This requires the corporate culture (set largely by an organisation's leader) to give staff the freedom to take ownership of their projects and to give them a sense of purpose in their role, whatever it may be. An excellent example of this concept is the response of a janitor sweeping the floor at NASA in 1962 when asked by President John F. Kennedy what he did. "I'm helping put a man on the moon."[58]

To ensure the due recognition and resources necessary to encourage people to be passionate, staff should be encouraged to trial new ideas and be allowed to make mistakes. Deloitte did an excellent study on how to install a passionate culture.[59] They propose three actionable ways that leaders can begin to cultivate a workforce that is ready and enthusiastic to step up to tomorrow's challenges:

1)   **Lead by example.**

As a leader, you need to be just that. Be passionate, find other passionate people and publicise their efforts. Show an acceptance of risk-taking and experimentation.

2)   **Provide focus.**

Define what matters for your staff (their purpose, impact, and role in the organisation) and where to direct their efforts. Encourage them to take ownership of projects and provide them with the space, latitude, and support to do that effectively.

3)   **Create the environment.**

If organisations are what they measure, they are also what they celebrate. Celebrate efforts that create knowledge that might lead to higher performance and eliminate any disincentives that prevent all but the bravest from taking risks. Rethink the way a group or unit is measured. Ensure the monitoring, recognition, and remuneration of staff are in line with the direction of the organisation. Encourage staff to develop by seeking challenges and working with others to learn. Progressively let these workgroups take on more responsibility and autonomy.

The whole movement for the importance of a positive mindset is associated with happiness, but it is actually talking about appreciation. As the line manager is often the greatest influence on whether people enjoy their work or not, you would expect that the promotion of staff would be carried out with the utmost care.

However, the problem for many companies is their promotion policy; people who are good at their jobs tend to get promoted. This means they may go from an area where they are experts to an area they know little about. This phenomenon is best summed up by the 1969 publication *The Peter Principle*, named after a concept proposed by Canadian educator Laurence J. Peter. According to this concept, employees are promoted based on their current progress, rather than for the skills and aptitude required for more senior roles. It results in people being promoted to the highest level of their incompetence.

In any domain, the best in the field are the ones usually promoted to a management position, often without training. New managers can become victims of being promoted beyond their capabilities and left to fester. In that situation, there is a massive loss of productivity and the unnecessary creation of much stress. Research carried out in the US showed that 87% of managers were promoted due to their success or expertise in a previous non-managerial role, or their longevity in the company. They wished they had more training. In this same study, companies failed to select the right candidate with the right mixture of talents 82% of the time.[60]

Governments are also wasting an enormous amount of money by not helping people find their passion. Most governments spend a fortune on education (around £100,000 - £140,000 per child), yet they spend next to nothing on helping students discover what they are actually passionate about. The associated loss in productivity is enormous. 50% of university graduates work in an area that is different from their university studies and 94% have changed jobs at least once by the age of 24.[61] Much more attention (and money) needs to be focused on helping students (particularly those aged between 16 and 22) to find what they are passionate about, to prevent these losses in potential.

It is well recorded that humans dislike wide or extensive choices due to the increased possibility of making the wrong selection, yet we are happy to leave our children to make one of the biggest decisions of their lives, and that too all alone.[62] We use the excuse that we are giving them the freedom to choose. But the selection process should be an integral part of the curriculum. Students need to be trained to find their work passions as part of the education process. They should follow methods to find out what they are passionate about. They should receive weekly training with a focus on what likes and dislikes they have had (and will have), and what they are good at.

Time and time again students (and often many adults) delegate their whole future to unknown human resources managers by sending out their CVs for every job they can find, hoping they will strike it lucky. Not only is this a massive waste of time for the applicant and the selector, but it also leads to bad selections, ones where people take a job for the money. Then, when they find they are not content, they are too scared to change, in case they can't find another job. The wastage in productivity and people's lives is astronomical.

It's important for everyone to find a role in life. Nearly everyone wants fulfilment in their lives, a sense of purpose, a way of helping their community. From a personal point of view, the sense of fulfilment comes from the appreciation of the things that are important to you. Unfortunately, many people feel that their work is pointless and plays little role in society. Making sure your staff can see and appreciate the role they play in the big picture will do much to give them a sense of importance, identity and satisfaction.

Fear: the brake on value creation

Fear is the ultimate brake on taking, repeating, or recommending (TRR) an action. If quality is confidence in an outcome for an acceptable period into the future, fear is the lack of confidence in an outcome. When it comes to decision-making, quality is the opposite to fear. It is an expectation that there is no way to exceed expectations.

We define confidence over time as a continued excess over expectations for an acceptable duration. Generally, we use the term 'quality' to imply confidence in a product and 'trust' to imply confidence when referring to an interaction. Confidence, quality, and trust are therefore essential elements of value creation. They result in consistent reactions from management, suppliers, and customers.

Confidence in the outcome is an essential part of making a decision. Without confidence (or with insufficient amounts of it), there is a sense of unease, leading to a reticence, unwillingness, or fear of making/taking a decision.

Fear results from the release of cortisol from the brain. High-level fear inhibits action, and long-term exposure to cortisol through constant stress results in a breakdown in decision-making capability. Frequent stress can increase the blood sugar level, leading to an overreaction to perceived threats and the inability to 'shut off'.[63] Fear comes about through either an excess of control and extreme boredom at not achieving anything or an excessive lack of control and an inability to achieve anything. Either way, if we are afraid, our expectations will be that we are incapable of achieving a goal, so we will be unwilling to TRR the action. The region of the brain called the midbrain tegmentum signals aversive events and inhibits midbrain dopamine neurons.[64] As highlighted earlier in Chapter

1, if dopamine is not produced, there is no value sensation or willingness to TRR the action.

Short-term exposure to fear results in the release of adrenalin from the adrenal gland (called the 'fight or flight' hormone). It prepares the body for facing or escaping the threat. While it is excellent at enabling the body to take either option, it is extremely demanding over the long term.[65]

Non-constructive criticism and condescension can create fear and destroy value

The worst thing we can do to someone is to ridicule them. It highlights the limits a person has created for themselves, which are there because the person feels out of control beyond their self-imposed barrier. Criticism (unless provided in a constructive and positive manner) diminishes a person's output and hence destroys value.

Ridicule and criticism put pressure on people to make a decision beyond their person's limits. It usually comes from someone that is capable of doing a task, and who is not intimidated by their own limit. However, it is highly destructive for two reasons. Firstly, it diminishes someone's efforts, and secondly, it is highly likely the person on the receiving end will attempt to carry out an activity beyond their capabilities. This can result in further mistakes and more prohibitive fear.

Chapter 7

How and why we
make decisions

Every time we make a decision or choice, there is a risk. It doesn't matter how many times we have taken the decision before, there is always the risk (however small) of the unexpected happening. This is why humans are not keen on too much choice.[66] If we offer more than a few options for our customers, the potential buyer becomes intimidated, because it increases the possibility of not making the right choice. That is why shops only display a few of their best examples. Some items are emphasised to limit the number of decision-making options.

A decision is an act of faith

A decision is an act of faith; we relinquish control of our current situation in the hope that we will improve our circumstances. Before a reasonably important decision, we assess the importance of the consequences and the likelihood of the predicted result. We evaluate the risks and the rewards. How much we carry out this process depends on our discipline and willingness to carry out a full evaluation, our willingness to take risks, how much relevant experience we have, and the consequences of making an error. We evaluate the cost vs. benefits.

If the decision is perceived as not very important (i.e., low risk, few consequences, a generally predictable outcome), little time and resources are applied to the process. In fact, in some situations, we can just 'dive' into making a decision without any consideration of the consequences.

However, a common factor in all decisions is the amount of control we feel and how we react to it. A balanced sense of control is essential if people are to make decisions. We know that control (although desirable) is often contrary to progression and success, so we do the minimum to get by. This suggests why 43% of the population is bored at work.[67]

Control and the power pendulum

To understand how we react to control, I have created what I call 'the power pendulum' (see over the page). It illustrates that how we react, and why, during the decision-making process depends significantly on our sense of control). Control is about finding the balance between too much, and too little. To the left of the pendulum, we have an increasing sense of control. To the right, we have decreasing control. When you are requested to carry out an action, if you have total control of the outcome, you feel you are learning nothing, you start getting bored, then you become frustrated, then you become annoyed, and finally, you give up.

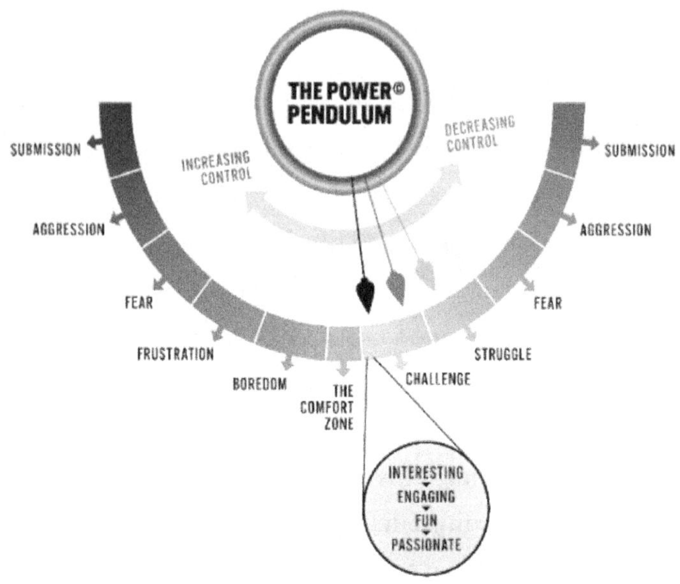

The levels of fear on either side of the pendulum increase, indicating a profound dislike of the situation, and, where possible, a desire to avoid a repetition of it in the future. Your emotions and reactions are focused on the entity imposing the control. The sense of control is a result of your perception of influencing the task outcome. The weight of the pendulum pulls to the bottom where we feel comfortable. However, this is not ideal, as we are wired to want to operate slightly to the right to learn. Just how far to the right depends on an individual's capacity and desire to take risks. The motivation is to improve our capabilities to expand our areas of control so that we can enhance our ability to survive.

Our reactions to too much control

When we do a task where we have increasing (too much) control, or when we make an interaction/transaction we have done before, we know the outcome, so we tend to want to change or stop the activity. For example, if we purchase the same items, we might feel safe/comfortable, but if we keep buying them, we will get bored. The more control (assurance of the outcome) that we have above being comfortable (to the left of the lowest point) the greater the reaction. Initially, we will feel bored with the process we are asked to carry out; if we have done it many times before, the reaction is even stronger, we know exactly what the outcome will be and it will be a repeat of the previous cycle of frustration and giving up.

The trouble is, that once brought to the extreme, fear is coded into the brain. The person is highly reticent to expose themselves to a similar situation. The willingness to do an activity or make positive decisions in this area is greatly diminished. A good example of this is in a corporate meeting or in a conversation where we are not learning anything. We start by yawning and doing displacement activities such as playing with our pens. The more we feel we are wasting our time, the stronger the reaction and the less willing we must expose ourselves to a similar situation. By definition, if making decisions and carrying out interactions that will be appreciated is creating value; anything that inhibits us from making decisions that we will appreciate is therefore inhibiting the creation of value.

The consequences of an excess of control

The response networks associated with stress overlap extensively with our memory and reward circuitry. This allows stress responses to be coloured by our prior experience and expected outcomes. The more excessive control of the outcome, the more we react to bring that level of control down. The stress circuit of the brain makes us react to get out of the increasingly frustrating situation. Repetitive or prolonged exposure to too much control can create much stress, illness, and dissatisfaction. The lack of a sense of ownership, purpose and contribution leads to disengagement.

The costs in terms of absenteeism from work and lost productivity are enormous (£340 billion per annum).[68] Employees need a balance, constant challenge. Too much control creates frustration and disengagement.[69]

The comfort zone and progressively releasing control

If we move to the right side of the pendulum, we pass the lowest point of the pendulum. The comfort zone is naturally where we gravitate because we are reasonably sure of the outcome. There is little risk, but we feel we are not progressing, pushing the barriers, or increasing our capabilities. As we move further right, we also have decreasing control. It starts off being interesting, we are taking little in the way of risk, and we feel that we are pushing the limits and learning something new. The interaction/transaction is interesting or fun. Having fun or being passionate about the task is the point where you still have optimum control when you are pushing the limits. There is no unwanted loss of control. This zone is where we are the most productive. We have the optimum amount of control and interest.

As we move beyond this point, we are less sure of the outcome. The decision and its consequences are a challenge. We can keep this up for a limited time before we must drop back to a less stressful situation. For example, the person (or situation) may be unreliable or react in a manner that we don't understand or agree with.

The next stage moving right is when the task becomes a struggle. For example, we may have difficulty understanding the (re)actions of the individual or organisation we're dealing with. We will remain in this stage until we can extract ourselves from the situation. Having experienced this state once, we will tend to avoid similar interactions/transactions in the future.

Beyond this struggle stage, the loss of control becomes excessive. The interaction/transaction becomes irrational or uncontrollable. Fear sets in, and a stress reaction occurs, that is coded into the brain.[70] This will make us avoid that situation/person at all costs.

The balance of control is critical when people are required to make decisions. At the workplace, people need to operate in that critical zone between interest and passion. When looking at the findings of the Gallup Q^{12} engagement survey about what people are looking for at work, productivity is largely determined by where people are positioned on the pendulum. For example, do they have the support and tools they feel are necessary to carry out their job? If they do, they feel sufficiently in control of what they are trying to achieve. Other key indicators include whether they find their efforts rewarding, do they feel their job gives them the opportunity to do what they feel they are best at, whether in the last six months has someone talked to them about their progress, and how they are pushing their capabilities.

Chapter 8

How we should measure the value creation inside our organisations

Measuring the value that we are missing under the current accounting and economic system (i.e., value + expectations, or 'appreciation') is easier than you might think. In fact, we have the solution right in front of us.

Simply ask people, market researchers have been doing it for years.

American psychologist and management guru, Rensis Likert, invented a simple measurement method when doing his PhD back in 1932.[71] He used it to capture the extent of a person's attitudes and feelings towards international affairs. The 5-star Likert scale he developed is now very useful in conducting surveys. It has applications in mass marketing for measuring customer satisfaction, as well as in the social sciences for attitude-related research projects.

It can also be used to capture our assessment of intangible value.

Using the Likert system to measure intangible value

For example, when we use a service such as a hotel or a restaurant, we are often asked for our opinion of the experience. We can also voluntarily offer our opinion online via social media platforms or Google reviews. We click from one to five stars, and we send our review. We think we have just sent our opinion on the quality of the service (which we have), but we have also recorded our assessment of intangible value. The organisation Renzi's collecting the review receives the rating (e.g., the hotel, restaurant, social media platform or Google) and will create an average which it will post and publicise. Our opinion or rating will then have an influence on the behaviour of future potential customers (i.e., their willingness to interact or make a decision). They will tend to buy/select the higher-rated service and convert the intangible into a tangible valuation.

However, as explained earlier in the book, the true definition of value (and what is currently being overlooked in our measurement system) is "the appreciation of the excess over expectations". Our opinion or appreciation actually gives an implicit assessment of value or the worth of something. It requires us to ponder how much we appreciate a decision choice, as well as how much choice we are willing to relinquish to buy a particular good or to experience a particular service. Money is simply the right to make a choice.

Initially, the suggested Likert rating system of appreciation will simply be relative; how much one place, decision, interaction, or transaction is preferred over another. However, with time and enough data, the system will generate an absolute figure. For example, it will be able to determine that a restaurant/hotel with a 4.8-star rating in a typical location and with a specific type of service will earn X thousand per month or year. This will be able to be compared to the earnings of a similar service with a 3.8-star rating. We will be able to determine that for every 0.1 increase in star rating (be that a percentage or a figure increase), the organisation will earn X amount or have Y additional turnover. The stars will take on their own precise value. As more and more data is gathered, the value of each characteristic valued by the customer will become apparent. For example, hotels will be able to determine how factors such as a good view, a riverside location or ensuite bathrooms add to their customers' evaluation. The assessment could even be taken down to micro levels of value such as the hotel giving away free soaps and shampoo or having paper toilet seat covers available.

The Likert scale is a relative and absolute measurement system for evaluating value. It assesses real value as perceived by the customer, unlike the commercial or financial assessment (a near-constant average price that is just a seller's one-off, best guess of highly variable and subjective customer needs). The relative and absolute nature of the Likert rating system also enables it to be used to assess true value in just about any context. It can be used in any situation where we have an opinion on something important, to gauge our level of support or disagreement. It could therefore be used equally well in both commercial and non-commercial organisations.

It would be especially useful for both for-profit and not-for-profit organisations, where aspects of (or all) of their operations are not financially measured by current systems. Most of the value changes of products and services occur outside the narrow perspective of the current measurement system. However, under the Likert system of measurement, if you can rate something, you can value it. It could therefore be applied to value the productive output of anyone doing just about any task for the good of others, that they may, or may not, know.

Monetising the hidden value in the economy

The 'killer app' with this proposed system is that it can be used to define success in other forms besides financial. It puts both not-for-profit and for-profit organisations on the same measurement scale.

We could use this system to manage the vast quantities of value being created that, currently, goes unseen. It makes little sense to measure value just once when there is a whole chain of events that both lead up to, and follow on from the point of sale.

The suggested Likert system would be particularly relevant in non-commercial organisations where there is no point of sale. 'Customers' can be asked to evaluate the productive output of anyone using the Likert system. The teacher, doctor, nurse, civil servant, soldier, policeman, librarian, museum curator, home carer, 'back office ', etc. can all be evaluated/appreciated. Assuming there is enough data to create provable correlations, the relative and absolute assessment of their value can be determined. The system would measure the productive output of everyone in real-time, everywhere. In fact, any rating system will work (including the Net Promoter Score, except that it would require more manipulation of data than a simple Likert scale).

It is important to remember that the focus of the suggested system is the appreciated (valued) aspects of output. The system ratings by customers should be positive, and criticism should be constructive. Criticism should only be provided if a correction is required, and customers (or anybody) providing this criticism should focus on the issue (not the person).

Converting appreciation into monetary terms

So, if we can measure value (appreciation), how do we convert it into monetary terms? We have to establish the downstream financial consequences of people's actions. If there is insufficient data available, the key performance indicators of individuals can be determined and cross-correlated downstream for their financial consequences.

The stars could also be used as a form of corporate currency, whereby everyone is allocated a specific number of stars to show their gratitude to other employees for their additional, or supplementary efforts. The stars allocated by voters could then be used as part of the organisation's remuneration system. To stop statistical distortions, extreme votes (if below a certain quantity) could be excluded, as there is usually somebody that has a negative view on whatever output someone has produced. A person's collection of 'thank you' stars could be cashed in at the corporate 'shop' and exchanged for 'gifts' such as experience days out, household gadgets, or special nights out in a hotel.

There are lots of assessment and/or monitoring systems available on the market that could be used as alternatives to the star system. The key is extending their current use, so as to carefully collect and analyse data in a way that information on the appreciation (value) generated at all levels of an organisation can be determined.

Chapter 9

Tying the rating system into a blockchain (and why you should)

The simplicity and power of the 5-star rating system are amplified when attaching it to a blockchain. Blockchains enable the indelible recording of the value transfer of productive output. In other words, they supply permanent proof of the creation and recognition of value. There is a clear record of the date, amount, parties involved, and the exact amount exchanged. Every participant in the blockchain can see and verify every interaction/transaction that takes place. A blockchain system is therefore completely transparent.

The blockchain record of each interaction/transaction is equal to its underlying value, which is crucial to maintaining equilibrium in the economy. Using a blockchain to measure value would enable a central bank to know the exact demand for money, hence helping better balance the money supply. A balanced money supply in turn avoids currency over/undersupply scenarios that create the problems of inflation and deflation. A blockchain could act as a basis for corporate, regional, national, and even global, money supply. It ensures that digital money is transferred, along with the right to make a choice.

In effect, a blockchain system is a digital equivalent of the 'one use and pass on' system that is a characteristic of cash. This 'one use and pass on' characteristic has to be imposed, otherwise, any person or organisation can keep 'spending the same money over and over again'. The banking system is very careful to balance out the gain of the right to choose (given to the recipient of the money) with the equal and opposite loss (i.e., the removal of that right from the sender). This was why, historically, it often took days for banks to transfer money.

But with today's computing power, this cross-checking of the transfer of rights can be done in microseconds. In fact, this is one of the current issues of using blockchain technology. The current banking system allows tens of thousands of transfers to be done every second, while blockchains can rarely exceed hundreds per second. The good news is, blockchain technology is not even a decade old, and its speed is rapidly increasing. Banking systems, on the other hand, have been developing for far longer. However, Ripple believes its blockchain technology is already capable of a transaction rate of 50 000 per second, which is twice the rate of the best banking system.[72]

Under the current mainstream digital currency system, more 'rights to choose' can be artificially created (by banks), than there are product/service solutions on the market. When this happens, the supply of money exceeds the productive capacity of the economy, and inflation occurs. When inflation occurs, people lose purchasing power. Blockchain technology can avoid this problem from happening. Due to the permanent and transparent nature of blockchain transactions, it restores the 'one use and pass on principle' that underpins both the value and supply of money.

Below is a made-up story of how this 'one use and pass on' principle works with cash, and why it's so important that it be maintained in our digital currency era using blockchain technology.

A lady arrives at a hotel one evening and is asked to leave a £50 note deposit at reception as a guarantee. The lodger then goes to her hotel room. The receptionist takes the £50 and nips around the corner to pay the butcher for the last month's meat. The butcher receives the note in payment and then drives to the countryside to pay the farmer the £50 for the lamb he bought last week. The farmer then takes the £50 and drives into town and meets the harvesting contractor in the pub to pay him £50 for the combining work he did during the summer. The harvesting contractor goes to the neighbouring village and uses the £50 to pay for last season's fertilizer usage. Before breakfast the next morning, the fertilizer salesperson nips into the hotel to pay off his company's outstanding lodging bill and pays the receptionist with the same £50 note. The receptionist then puts the same £50 note deposit back in the hotel kitty. After breakfast, the lodger pays her hotel bill and reclaims the same £50 she deposited the night before, unaware of the journey carried out by the note in the last 12 hours.

The above example shows that the transfer of money simply represents the transfer of the right to choose. That right is not affected by the number of times it is used. The right remains the same. When you have cash (notes and coins), you have the right to choose up to the value you have. That right continues for the holder of the cash, no matter how many times it is transferred.

The example is also an excellent explanation of the velocity of money (also known as the transaction rate). To carry out all the transactions required just one £50 note if any one of the individuals decided to keep the money (for example, to buy another asset), the (micro) economy would have been held up, as there wouldn't have been enough money circulating to enable all the transactions to take place. This is a major problem when wealth in society is concentrated in too few hands. Rich people tend to put their money into assets which reduces the velocity of money, while poor people tend to spend everything. This is an excellent justification to create a universal basic wage and to pay poorer people better, as it will enable more decisions to be made, and therefore more value to be created. The transaction rate increases the supply of money, without more money needing to be created and potentially creating an inflationary risk, and the more that money circulates (i.e., the more rights there are to make decisions), the larger the economy and the more everyone (both rich and poor) benefits.

Chapter 10

How you install this rating system in your organisation

Both large and small contributions in an organisation can be valuable and should be recognised. The timing of the measurement is also essential. Recognition needs to happen at the moment when it has the most potential impact, as the impact will fade over time.

Recognition should also be tied to the receiver's perception of value.[73] Money can be a nice gesture, but it isn't always the most effective means of showing your appreciation. It is important to make sure that the recognition given coincides with the values your team holds. Employee rewards don't have to be large or costly; in many cases, small rewards are more effective because they can be given more frequently, and frequency is a crucial element of a successful rewards program.

Peer-to-peer recognition software is essential to measure

the motivation and productive output of all members of an organisation. Stakeholders should use available software programs on an ongoing basis to accurately measure both.

Measuring motivation

Motivation increases employee engagement, which, in turn, increases productivity.[74] Motivation could be easily measured in one of two ways: first, to ask every staff member to rate their level of motivation at the end of each day. They could slide a marker along a scale from 1 (very demotivated) to 5 (extremely motivated). Each day they compare themselves against how they felt the previous day working for the organisation. Is it higher, the same or lower?

This measurement scale would keep a record of each staff member's level of motivation over time. If a person's level is deteriorating, this should alert the organisation's HR department to identify the cause and to take corrective action to improve the situation.

In addition, accumulating the measurement scores by team, group, section, or the organisation as a whole would give you an insight into the quality of leadership at each organisational level and whether leaders are motivating their staff.

The second way would be to conduct monthly staff engagement surveys. The 20 questions below have been developed using the Gallup Q[12] and the Culture Amp employee engagement surveys as a guide.[75,76] Both of these organisations survey millions of people all over the world about their work engagement levels. The questions are divided into six sections to gather information about how content and aligned staff are with their organisation and its goals. The first five sections could be answered using a 5-star rating system ranging from 'Strongly Agree' to 'Strongly Disagree'. Questions in the final section are open to encourage more detailed responses.

Work passion

1. Do you feel full of pride working for this organisation?

2. Do you recommend this company as a great place to work?

3. Do you rarely consider looking for another job?

4. Do you intend to stay in the organisation for at least two more years?

5. Does the organisational culture make you want to work more than you would in a similar job elsewhere?

Support levels

6. Do you have the resources you require to do your work well?

7. Do you have the necessary training and

---

development to do your work well?

8. Do most of the organisational processes and systems help you to achieve your objectives?

Alignment

9. Is it very clear what success is in your work?

10. Do you receive timely and appropriate recognition when you do a good job?

11. Are quality and improvement crucial aspects of the organisation's focus?

Development

12. Has management shown real support for your career?

13. Are there genuine opportunities and a future for you within the organisation?

14. Do you believe this is a great organisation to develop your career?

Management

15. Do the organisation's leaders keep everyone informed about what's going on?

16. Is your line manager a great example for staff?

17. Have the organisation's leaders communicated a

vision that gives you a sense of purpose?

Open questions

18. What are we doing really well in the organisation at the moment?

19. What areas could we improve on?

20. Is there something else we should have asked you about?

Measuring productive output

Once motivation has been measured, the other piece of the puzzle is measuring to measure productive output, using their KPIs, or Key Performance Indicators, which are the principal measures of someone's output. For example, for a secretary this would be calls taken per day, their ability to solve customer problems, the number of people they welcome each day and how visitors feel they are received. Each staff member should draw a diagram each month and follow the steps below:

Step 1: Write 'me' in the centre of a sheet of paper and put a circle around it.

Step 2: Draw a line to everybody they have dealt with as part of their job for the last month. They may be working with your organisation's customers, suppliers, etc.

Step 3: With the assistance of their line manager, they

should choose seven of the people who have received the most of their productive output over the month. The staff member should create a short description of how they add value to the other party. For example:

- For your **line manager**

"To carry out your KPIs to take the strain off your boss and give them more time to think, so you can both be successful in helping other members of the organisation."

- For an **external/internal supplier**

"To make the supply criteria as clear as possible and work with them to provide exactly what we need."

- For the **external/internal customer**

"To understand their needs and requirements and to communicate them clearly and succinctly to my organisation."

- For **those that support you**

"To keep them clearly informed of what is required and to provide timely recognition and appreciation of their support."

- For **those you support**

"To offer them the best of your knowledge and capabilities, and to coordinate your efforts with other supporters to enable those that you support to give their best.

Step 4: Send each of the seven people an electronic

"evaluation of output" form. The form should look something like this:

"Please, could you take the time to show your appreciation for the assistance/support/service I have given you over the past month, and indicate how much you appreciated our professional interaction".

The recipients would click on the relevant rating and their responses should be compiled into a central database for the staff member.

If the ratings were broken down to reflect the employee's KPIs, they would be even more valuable. The ratings of people in similar jobs in similar industries could also be compared. When people want to change jobs and an HR department wants to assess them, they will have a more accurate measure of a person's value.

Chapter 11

A global system for
a global society

Besides its simplicity, the other key advantage of the rating system is that it can be used to assess value in any organisation anywhere, anytime. It can also be adjusted for use across different levels of an organisation to glean the true or actual value output as perceived by their 'customers' (be they paying customers, employees, suppliers, financiers of the organisation or any other stakeholders that have an interest in and an opinion on the organisational output).

You may be familiar with Glassdoor, the employment review website. It provides employees with the opportunity to rate their experience with an employer, to the point that they can even rate the CEO of their organisation who should create implicit value by their productive output.

A quick study I carried out in 2020 looked at the

Glassdoor rating held by the CEOs of the FT100 UK companies, along with employee perceptions of their future prospects at those organisations. There was a clear and direct correlation between CEO ratings and employee perceptions. Not surprisingly, 5-star rated CEOs attract the best employees, suppliers, and customers to work for (or with) them, and are hence most likely to have the most motivated workforce. The findings confirmed a clear connection between CEO popularity and corporate success. As more data comes in, there will be an increasingly precise correlation between the star rating of the CEO, and both the actual and likely income generation and profitability of the organisation.

Now, if you can correlate the actual and likely corporate income generation and profitability of the CEO with enough data, you should be able to calculate the contribution of each person and role in a company with a similar measurement system like the one I proposed in Chapter 8. Every employee's interaction or decision regarding their productive output can potentially create or destroy value. We don't necessarily need to measure every interaction or decision, but we should measure the overall perception of each employee's productive output from both internal and external customers and suppliers. This will determine each employee's value output (contribution) to the organisation as a whole.

It's like 360° feedback on how much an employee's output is appreciated by recipients. Many organisations already collect this data to some extent, but it needs to be measured and analysed on a much more frequent and focused basis to be a true indicator of the value of the output. The system would show the value as, and when, it is created both inside, and outside, the organisation. It treats not-for-profit organisations in the same manner as commercial enterprises initially showing relative success across the variety of roles in an organisation and, eventually, absolute success. Any given role may be relatively perceived in financial terms, and with enough data, in terms of the actual absolute value of its output.

Assessing the productive output of a commercial CEO against a non-commercial CEO

Let's now use the 5-star rating scale to assess the value of a commercial CEO with the CEO of a hospital trust. We'll assume that the Key Performance Indicators of the commercial CEO are increasing shareholder value, turnover, profitability, and the motivation of the workforce, as well as generating favourable perceptions of him/her. The KPIs of the hospital trust CEO are improving patient cure rates per bed per annum, lowering average waiting times for acute and emergency care as well as non-essential services, ensuring the hospital operates within its annual budget, increasing staff motivation levels and creating good impressions of him/herself and the organisation.

Perceptions of the commercial CEO's value could be assessed via shareholder ratings on the 5-star scale. Shareholders could make an assessment of what criteria are most important to them, whether it be shareholder value, turnover, profitability, or how socially responsible they perceive the company to be. The perspectives of value may differ depending on the shareholder. For example, speculators, pension funds, and private investors each may have different perceptions of value. The quantity of the ratings obtained should be sufficient to provide a genuine view of different investor perspectives. Too few ratings could lead to the data obtained being biased. However, as the amount of ratings (and data) grows, any biases should be reduced or eliminated.

In the beginning, the value assessments of different stakeholders (shareholders, customers, suppliers, and employees) could be kept and summarised separately. Their perception among these different groups will progressively become apparent. They may be perceived as being more valuable by some groups than others. However, over time, and with enough data, an average rating of their true value (as measured by feedback from across all stakeholder groups) should be able to be obtained without biases. The CEO's stakeholders should include anyone that uses or benefits from their productive output.

With enough data, it should be possible to assess a commercial CEO's impact (or potential impact) on a company. For example, it could be determined that a CEO with:

- a rating of between 4 and 5,

- in a company in Y industry,

- with an annual turnover of X,

  and

- a team of employees with a motivation level measured at 3.2,

  could be expected to:

- increase the company's turnover by 15-20% per annum,

- raise the employee motivation to 4.1-4.3 over a year, and

- increase shareholder value by 5-6% per annum.

Now let's turn our attention to assessing the CEO of a National Health Service trust. The trust's directors, employees, and patients could be all asked to rate their appreciation of the productive output of the CEO. Each group may place differing importance on the CEO's various KPIs (cure rates, waiting times, operating efficiency, staff motivation levels, and CEO perception). Like they would be for the commercial CEO, these ratings would be relative at first, but, with time and enough data, the rating system would become an absolute measure of financial and/or non-financial success.

For example, it may become apparent that a 4.8-star

rated CEO of a hospital trust is 40% more efficient in terms of budget savings, and creates staff motivation levels that are 1.5 times higher than a CEO with 3.4-star rating running a similar organisation.

Similarly, the productive output of government CEOs can be evaluated by stakeholders in all the different 'markets' served by their not-for-profit organisations: employees, customers (the end-users of services), suppliers, etc. For example, ambassadors from the Foreign Commonwealth and Development Office lobby foreign governments on behalf of British companies and the British government. Data can be compiled on which ambassadors and embassies are more effective than others. For example, it may be determined that an ambassador with a 4.6-star rating will be 50% more effective at representing British interests than an ambassador with a 3.1-star rating. On the national security front, the financial value could be measured in terms of the cost savings of maintaining diplomatic relations, and not going to war.

Assessing the value of doctors

Doctors save people's lives and shorten their illnesses. Individual doctor ratings will reflect how well their patients perceive them to be doing their jobs. The financial consequences of doctors doing their job can also be correlated with the increase in productive output that happens as a result of their work.

For example, if a doctor saves a 20-year-old

motorcyclist's life, society will have gained 35 years of productive output. Based on the average current gross annual salary of £36 611, that's a gross downstream value of £1.28 million. Obviously, the motorcyclist's full future earnings cannot be allocated to the doctor's work, also, tax and the cost of treatment would need to be deducted to determine the net value gain to society. However, this example gives you an idea of the value of doctors to society. Their remuneration should be connected to the value they indirectly help to create.

Assessing the value of the teaching profession

Teachers also create significant downstream value with the work that they do. Research indicates that top-performing teachers add 10 to 20% to the lifetime earnings of their students. In the US, that's equivalent to $400,000 per teacher per class per year. How many teachers get paid anything like that?[77,78] Measuring the future earnings of students and correlating that information with quality teaching would enable good teachers to demand a significant pay rise.

On the flip side, it has been proven that poor-performing teachers can destroy just as much value, if not more, as good teachers create. A rating system that includes the future earnings of pupils could be used to offer retraining, or the redeployment of these teachers to another occupation.

Everyone has an opinion on what constitutes a good or a bad teacher. Even from a young age, we all know a good teacher when we have one. The ideal characteristics of a good teacher should be determined by questioning students and parents, and correlating this information with student well-being and future earnings for up to twenty years after they leave school.

With today's computing power and big data analysis, it should be feasible to identify the top 10% of teachers and their common characteristics, such as their:

- fundamental approach to teaching,

- level of classroom discipline,

- understanding of their subject,

- passion for teaching,

- kindness (facilitating well-being),

- ability to make learning fun,
  and

- teaching effectiveness.

In terms of students rating their teachers, there may be error bias due to the age of the student. For example, 7-year-olds would be more likely to choose kinder teachers rather than more academically demanding ones. Another issue is that the further we go back in the history of the pupil, the more difficult it would be to determine the effect of only one teacher over the course of a student's future earnings. It would probably be best to focus on the final four to five years of school in terms of correlating earnings with teacher quality, as well as the length of time each teacher taught a particular student. This should enable the most influential teachers to be identified.

There could also be a potential issue in terms of measuring the relative improvement in a student that's attributable to their teacher. This issue could be overcome by developing a national metric to determine the motivation and capabilities of a class and how much support each student has from home. Each class could be assessed a couple of times a year and measured against set criteria to develop a class 'facility of learning' score that compares student ability levels at the start of the year versus those at the end.

It would make sense to create a national standard of the desired measurement range of top-performing teacher characteristics. Each characteristic would eventually acquire a value via measurement over time. Appreciation puts the value in value. For example, the value of a teacher that has a 4-star "passion for teaching rating" compared to one that has a 3-star rating would be reflected in their students' future salaries or star ratings in the workplace. Over time, it could be determined that students gain X amount for having a teacher with a Y star rating.

Profile tests could also be created to recruit and train better quality teachers so that the overall standard of the profession improves. This, in turn, will enhance the potential of students to create more value in their future careers. New and unassessed teachers who hold just some or all the characteristics will be able to be accurately valued almost from day one. There will be no need to wait for years to obtain the salaries of their students. Desirable teaching styles and characteristics could be reflected in productivity-related teacher salaries.

Ratings of heads of schools could also be correlated against factors such as the net improvement in overall student grades from one year to the next, as well as staff tenure and contentment level. Initially, the results will be relative, showing only the comparative merit of each head. However, over time, as the amount of data grows, the results will become an absolute measure. For example, they may show that a headteacher with a 4.7 rating will have a 50% higher pass rate among students, a 60% reduction in the dropout rate, 20% higher future student earnings, and 45% happier staff than a teacher with a 3.3 rating. The difference in value creation could be reflected in teacher salaries.

Assessing the downstream value of a not-for-profit organisation

Let's further illustrate the concept of downstream value creation by applying the system to a not-for-profit organisation: a social bakery, such as Big River Bakery, Newcastle upon Tyne. Let's assume that the bakery produces bread for paying customers as well as additional free bread for poor customers. They also employ people that face complex employment barriers. Both poor people and the workers could rate their appreciation of the bakery.

The downstream value creation for society could include:

- food equality for poorer people, allowing them to allocate their limited resources to more important items.

- skills-based training for staff working at the bakery, avoiding unemployment costs, and providing these workers with a sense of pride, self-esteem and improved quality of life.

- less hungry, aggressive, and unskilled people roaming the streets, avoiding the associated social costs.

- giving the social elite an understanding of the importance and role of social justice and well-being.

- working with charities, NGOs, and other social businesses as consultants, partners, and facilitators to deliver mutual goals.

- becoming an integral part of community well-being.

- working with schools on curriculum enrichment. For example, involving students in the baking process.

- working with the corporate sector in planning and delivering social innovation projects.

Chapter 12

The consequences for society

The appreciation rating system will enable all the value that is created in society to be measured more accurately and distributed more fairly. It will also make our workplaces nicer places to be. Value is being created and destroyed many times before and after the point of sale, and by measuring it at its various stages, we can manage it much better.

The system will measure 'how well employees at every level fulfil the expectations of the key people around them'. People will be truly and fairly assessed on their genuine contributions. The results will indicate the relative capability of each individual to fulfil the requirements of their role. Over time, the cumulative results will provide a range of potential earnings to match the value that a role is capable of producing. The group, or organisational level of success in terms of creating real value will also be obtained. The higher the rating, the greater the ability of the individual, group or organisation to fulfil the expectations of customers and/or suppliers.

The system will rank all individuals, groups, and organisations both relatively (for example, the top 5 in a domain) and absolutely (for example, a rating of X in this job will earn Y or generate an extra 100K turnover per month). Each relationship or interaction will have a value to the relevant individual and organisation (i.e., not a social value). The individual's value is their contribution to the success of the organisation. Sufficient data collection and analysis will enable the importance of an individual to an organisation to be identified and accurately remunerated.

The Likert rating system will show both the relative and absolute differences between one individual and another in a job role. It will also highlight each role's importance to the overall success of the organisation and hopefully give the person doing each role a sense of purpose. Those earning better ratings via additional effort will be quickly and proportionally rewarded, while those earning fewer positive ratings will be encouraged to work where they will be more appreciated, leading to places of work being much happier and fairer places to be.

Many areas and people in society are currently not formally measured, recorded, or properly valued for their contributions. This system gives a much more accurate assessment of value everywhere that it's created. Both the quantity of measured subjective value and the money supply will increase exponentially. Recording transactions on a blockchain can ensure that genuine value is permanently, and irrevocably, recorded. New currency will be created to match the value created.

Recording an overall impression of a person's productive output will provide a fairer assessment of their value added. Cumulatively, the same can be done to measure the value added by the organisation as a whole.

When we monetise all of this productive output, it means that society has to show gratitude by paying for it, so more money needs to be issued. However, this will not result in inflation, as the money being issued will be in direct proportion to the value being produced via the blockchain system. Initially, the organisation can 'pay' with tokens/gold stars allocated to managers and peers to thank their co-workers for their assistance. The key is to make the process frequent, rapid, and positive. It involves frequently saying thank you, as a person is doing a valuable activity so that they can associate the action with the reward. It also requires rapid evaluation via a peer-to-peer software system because people can't be expected to spend all their time evaluating others. Finally, it involves being positive because the very act of saying thank you is encouraging the other person to take, repeat or recommend (TRR) the valuable action and hence create more value.

The Likert system to measure appreciation will enable the not-for-profit organisation to be valued in the same way as a commercial organisation. There will be a greatly reduced differential between the 'haves' and the 'have nots',

the profit makers, and the not-for-profit organisations. It will make people realise the true value of what is being produced, rather than recording value in the crude, biased and misleading way we do at the moment.

No longer will the commercial and upper levels of society get a disproportionate share of the rewards. Vast quantities of society that at the moment are ignored because their value production is not (or badly) measured will instead be assessed according to the value they are creating for others. The appreciation system will remove much (if not all) poverty and provide the justification for introducing a universal basic wage for everyone, irrespective of their labour status.

Conclusion

Amajor consequence of this new paradigm is that we will express our appreciation on a much wider basis. The expression of our views will be positive, constructive, and supportive. People will be encouraged to seek out their true identity and work passions. Employees will be encouraged to innovate to both explore their capabilities and to express their identities through their work. They will know their strengths and will use them to better support those that depend on them. People will be much more aware of their capabilities, roles, and effects. They will play to their strengths and feel both recognised, as well as appreciated, for their efforts. Those that are critical, negative or depreciative will be quickly encouraged to work elsewhere.

For organisations, their costs will go down, their efficiency will increase, and their customers will be better served as employees innovate to improve their productive output. Shortfalls in knowledge, facilities, and support will be clearly and quickly identified and resolved. Workplaces will be more relaxed yet more customer-focused. Fairness and justice will be integral to the culture. People will have more flexibility in terms of where and how they work. An enhanced work/life balance should enable everyone to relax more. Accounting will be accurate, almost real-time, and predictive. Economics will be a fact and reality-based science, rather than based on theories and hypotheticals.

All that remains is to invite you to consider *Thankonomics* as a basis for reconsidering your concept of value, and all its consequences, to create a fairer, more equal, and just society.

If you want to know more about the concept or support the movement of *Thankonomics*, please visit the website at www.thankonomics.com. If you have enjoyed this book or like the concept please 'help the cause' by writing a positive review on the amazon Thankonomics page here

If you would like the author to present the concept to an audience, please send an email to enquiries@thankonomics.com.

Glossary

Appreciation: The subjective pricing (determining the importance) of the excess over expectations. Appreciation is a fundamental motivator to take, repeat, and/or recommend a decision.

Asset: The accumulation of someone's (or some people's) productive output. An asset can be used by one or more people to collect and store the potential to release appreciation.

Confidence: The belief that the expected outcome will occur, and continue to do so, for the foreseeable future. It is a form of subjective value.

Control: The assurance of an outcome.

Decision: The selection of an option (usually with the intention of improving your situation) and the momentary release of control (because there is always a doubt, however small, of the outcome).

Expectations: The subjective minimum to justify making a decision.

Fear: Loss of control and the expectation that you will be incapable of achieving your goal. Fear is the ultimate brake (inhibitor) to taking, repeating, or recommending an action. The opposite to passion.

Money: A society-wide agreement to accept a tool that is supposed to equate to value as a method of exchange. It provides you with the right to make alternative measured choices up to the perceived level of your prior contribution of productive output to society.

Numerical value: A number/digit/amount.

Passion: The ultimate long-term motivation, almost 100% intrinsic. Passionate people have little or no expectations, they achieve maximum excess and value creation.

Price: the amount of choice or resources (i.e., the facilities to carry out choices such as time, money, and expertise) that a buyer is willing to concede or commit to make a purchase acquisition or to have an interaction.

Productive output: The elements of one's life that are committed to carrying out an activity for someone else, that we may or may not know. In return, we expect appreciation in terms of recognition and the ability to make choices in other areas to the perceived value of our output.

Quality: A term of respect usually applied to a product, but it can be applied to a service. It is the perceived excess over expectations that will occur and continue for an acceptable time in the future. It can be used as a synonym of value. As it is an excess over expectations, quality is a form of subjective value. It encourages decision-making.

Recognition: The expression of appreciation in public or, at least, in front of other people.

Subjective value: The excess over expectations. It is represented in the brain by a highly agreeable and appreciated discharge of dopamine down the reward pathway into the Nucleus Accumbens. The discharge is proportional to the perceived excess over expectations. The sensation of value is a fundamental motivator to making decisions that appear to have the potential to improve our situation. The strength or appreciation of that feeling determines our willingness to repeat or recommend decisions.

Trust: A term usually applied to a service or interaction indicating that the perceived excess over expectations will occur and continue for the length of the relationship. As it is an excess over expectations, it is a form of subjective value. It encourages decision-making.

Value in value: The appreciation (recognition, or acknowledgment) of the excess over expectations, plus expectations, themselves.

Wealth: the accumulation of the right to choose. It inhibits the right to exercise the right to choose and therefore limits the economy. It has the same effect as a tax, except the beneficiary is the accumulator, not the government.

About the author

Andrew Robshaw has spent more than 30 years influencing international companies across Latin America and Europe. He is a Sloan Fellow with a Master of Science in Business Strategy and Administration (London Business School), a Master of Science in Bio-aeronautics (Cranfield Institute of Technology) and, a Bachelor of Science (Nottingham University).

He started his working life as a trainee commodity trader before he set up and ran a successful trans-European logistics company based in France. During his career, he has run three bi-national Chambers of Commerce in Chile (British, Australian and Norwegian). He has also provided strategy, international business, and market development advice to companies of all sizes throughout South America and Europe.

Andrew has been applying his extensive experience of 'thinking outside the box' as a new economy investigator, and lecturer for several years. He helps organisations to be more productive, efficient, and most of all, more appreciative.

He is passionate about the principles behind this book and the need for a radical paradigm shift in the global economy. He hopes it will transform the world into a fairer, more just, beneficial, and appreciative place for all. It is the culmination of years of research, observation, and practical experience.

Andrew has always enjoyed life, learning, adventure, and sports, having been a keen hang glider pilot, free-fall parachutist, and trampolinist. He has also completed a London Marathon.

In 2009 he was diagnosed with Parkinson's disease, and this changed his whole perspective. He resumed his writing and research, which he understood as his life's mission. Post-diagnosis, Andrew has continued to chase his dreams. He has learned to surf and paraglide, as well as continuing as a keen mountain biker and skier. He holds the firm belief that nothing is impossible.

Acknowledgements

Jessica Pryce-Jones:

How can I thank you enough for your brilliant mind, profound insights, and unwavering support?

Bridgit Temple:

Thank you for introducing me to the CEO of a major Swiss company. You and Jessica were able to see the importance of this book's concepts way ahead of time.

David Shukman:

The brilliant BBC reporter who had the vision to have utter belief in his wife's judgment and to give his time and full commitment to supporting her initiatives. You are an example for us all.

Jocelyn Ireson-Paine:

Thank you for taking my ideas and turning them into software that was truly way ahead of its time. The programs you produced would not look out of place today, despite being written 20 years ago.

Jaime Ramsden:

Another brilliant mind who was willing to spend hours discussing the concepts in this book when they were just hunches for me. Thanks for keeping in touch all these years and always being willing to review the latest development on this book.

Maja Adenborg:

How can I thank you enough? Commuting every day to apply your razor-sharp intellect and ability to break down common themes, to help me think seriously outside of the box, and to tirelessly question my logic with constructive but incisive observations. You reflect Sweden at its best!

Marthe Selas:

For reading through the text and supporting me at the Norwegian Chamber of Commerce.

Jon Baker:

Over many years, always willing to read through the book's ideas and drafts to give gentle, but well-considered feedback.

Andy Haddon:

Thank you for your efforts in including my project with yours.

Cornelius Greyling:

You heard about my ideas in a random conversation and immediately recognised their significance. You had the courage to introduce me to a large multinational software company.

Ramon Burr, Tom Warwick and Tina Hamilton:

Thanks for introducing me to your organisation.

Sloan 2000 (London Business School):

Special thanks also to Richard Allen, Jean Christophe Bedos, Rebecca Churchill, Barbara Domayne-Hayman, Keith Gubbins, Caja Klabbers, Steve Kowal, Amanda Leness, Jonathan Lloyd-Plat, Rohit Milstein, Lester Pereira, Bijorn Smid-Olsen, Anne Saunders and Sarah Seedsman. You are all part of that amazing and most intelligent group I know, and each of you was willing to support this 'entrepreneur with a mission' in your own way.

Neurosurgery Team (Newcastle Royal Infirmary):

To the most amazing example of non-registered value added. Lead by Neurosurgeon Alistair Jenkins and driven by the Specialist Clinical Nurse Una Brechany they inserted two probes deep into my brain, connecting them to a pacemaker and gave me back my life.

The British National Health Service:

Since my return to the UK, this amazing institution has created value beyond recognition for me personally by working tirelessly through the Pandemic for the entire nation. If ever there was an excuse to change the current assessment of value, this is it. The NHS is a major creator of value and is one of the country's greatest assets, it should not be accounted for as an expense.

John Coomer (Editor):

Thank you for having the patience to filter through the unintelligible jumble of many years of reflection and bring it into a logical, comprehensible format, whilst gently bringing me to order for my more tenuous claims.

Joanna Penn:

Although we have never met nor spoken, your course on the elements of writing a book was as complete as they were interesting. A must for any budding author.

Rodrigo Eterovic:

Thank you for having the vision in the early years of this project, being my first commercial customer, for being around throughout the development of the concept, and for quietly supporting me through the dark years.

Charles and Maureen Robshaw:

Thank you to my parents for the wonderful example they provided. Just how did you get the time to do all the things you did?

Paul Robshaw, Anna Lewis, and Helen Smith:

Thank you to my long-suffering siblings for quietly being there to support me and helping me to dig myself out of the innumerable holes I have dug for myself.

Sebastian, Natasha, Pascual, and Lucas:

A lifetime of thanks to my four ever-patient and wonderful

children.

Marcela Núñez Aguilar:

A massive thank you to my partner for providing tireless support. Without you, this book would never have been written.

Endnotes

[1] Gibson, B., Wilson, D. J., Feil, E., & Eyre-Walker, A. (2018). The distribution of bacterial doubling times in the wild. *Proceedings. Biological sciences, 285*(1880)

[2] Schultz W. (2004). Neural coding of basic reward terms of animal learning theory, game theory, microeconomics and behavioural ecology. Current opinion in neurobiology, 14(2), 139–147. https://doi.org/10.1016/j.conb.2004.03.017

[3] Schultz, W., Carelli, R. M., & Wightman, R. M. (2015). Phasic dopamine signals: from subjective reward value to formal economic utility. *Current opinion in behavioral sciences, 5*, 147–154. https://doi.org/10.1016/j.cobeha.2015.09.006 https://www.ncbi.nlm.nih.gov/pmc/articles/PMC4692271/

[4] Berridge K. C. (2007). The debate over dopamine's role in reward: the case for incentive salience. *Psychopharmacology, 191*(3), 391–431. https://doi.org/10.1007/s00213-006-0578-x https://pubmed.ncbi.nlm.nih.gov/17072591/

[5] Schott BH1, Minuzzi L, Krebs RM, Elmenhorst D, Lang M, Winz OH, Seidenbecher CI, Coenen HH, Heinze HJ, Zilles K, Düzel E, Bauer A (2008) Mesolimbic functional magnetic resonance imaging activations during reward anticipation correlate with reward-related ventral striatal dopamine release journal of neuroscience 24 December 2008, 28 (52) 14311-14319 ; DOI: https://doi.org/10.1523/JNEUROSCI.2058-08.2008

https://www.ncbi.nlm.nih.gov/pubmed/18

[6] Schultz W., Dayan P., Montague R. R. (1997). A neural substrate of predict and reward. Science 275, 1593–1599

[7] Hollerman JR, Schultz W (1998) Dopamine neurons report an error in the temporal prediction of reward during learning. Nat Neurosci. 1998 Aug; 1(4):304-9. [PubMed] https://pubmed.ncbi.nlm.nih.gov/10195164/

[8] Bayer, H., & Glimcher, P. (2005). Midbrain Dopamine Neurons Encode a Quantitative Reward Prediction Error Signal. Neuron, 47(1), 129-141. doi:10.1016/j.neuron.2005.05.020

[9] Levy, D., & Glimcher, P. (2012). The root of all value: a neural common currency for choice. Current Opinion in Neurobiology, 22(6), 1027-1038. doi:10.1016/j.conb.2012.06.001

[10] Saxe and Haushofer (2018). For love or money: a common neural currency for social and monetary reward. - PubMed - NCBI . Ncbi.nlm.nih.gov. Retrieved 19 November 2018

[11] Tremblay L, Schultz W. Relative reward preference in primate orbitofrontal cortex. Nature. 1999 Apr 22;398(6729):704-8. doi: 10.1038/19525. PMID: 10227292

[12] Elliott, R., Agnew, Z., & Deakin, J. F. W. (2008). Medial orbitofrontal cortex codes relative rather than absolute value of financial rewards in humans. *European Journal of Neuroscience, 27*(9), 2213-2218. https://doi.org/10.1111/j.1460-9568.2008.06202.x

[13] Beza C. (2014): The Nucleus Accumbens the core valuation region. https://www.youtube.com/watch?v=StxdPsmx744

[14] Schultz W. (2016). Dopamine reward prediction error coding. *Dialogues in clinical neuroscience, 18*(1), 23–32. https://doi.org/10.31887/DCNS.2016.18.1/wschultz

[15] Bartra O, McGuire JT, Kable JW (2013)The valuation system: a coordinate-based meta-analysis of BOLD fMRI experiments examining neural correlates of subjective value. Neuroimage. 2013 Aug 1;76:412-27. doi: 10.1016/j.neuroimage.2013.02.063. Epub 2013 Mar 15 https://pubmed.ncbi.nlm.nih.gov/23507394/

[16] Lieberman,Eisenberger (2009) Pains and Pleasures of social life https://www.scn.ucla.edu/pdf/Lieberman%20&%20Eisenberger%20(2009)%20Science.pdf

[17] Izuma, K, Daisuke. S, Norihiro,(2008) Processing of Social and Monetary Rewards in the Human Striatum VOLUME 58, ISSUE 2, P284-294, APRIL 24, 2008 0.1016/j.neuron.2008.03.020

[18] Grabenhorst, F., & Rolls, E. T. (2011). Value, pleasure and choice in the ventral prefrontal cortex. *Trends in cognitive sciences, 15(2), 56–67.* https://doi.org/10.1016/j.tics.2010.12.004

[19] Abler, B., Walter, H., Erk, S., Kammerer, H., & Spitzer, M. (2006, 06). Prediction error as a linear function of reward probability is coded in human Nucleus Accumbens. *NeuroImage, 31*(2), 790-795. doi:10.1016/j.neuroimage.2006.01.001 https://www.ncbi.nlm.nih.gov/pubmed/16487726

[20] Berridge K. C. (2012). From prediction error to incentive salience: mesolimbic computation of reward motivation. *The European Journal of Neuroscience, 35* (7), 1124–1143. https://doi.org/10.1111/j.1460-9568.2012.07990. https://pubmed.ncbi.nlm.nih.gov/22487042/

[21] Rilling J. K., Gutman D. A., Zeh T. R., Pagnoni G., Berns G. S., Kilts C. D. (2002). A neural basis for social cooperation. Neuron 35, 395–40510. 1016/S0896-6273(02)00755-9 [PubMed] https://pubmed.ncbi.nlm.nih.gov/12160756/

[22] Kringelbach M. L. (2005). The human orbitofrontal cortex: linking reward to hedonic experience. Nat. Rev. Neurosci. 6, 691–70210.1038/nrn1747 [PubMed] https://pubmed.ncbi.nlm.nih.gov/16136173/

[23] Peters, J., & Büchel, C. (2010). Neural representations of subjective reward value. *Behavioural Brain Research*, 213(2), 135–141.

[24] Izuma, K, Daisuke. S, Norihiro,(2008) Processing of Social and Monetary Rewards in the Human Striatum VOLUME 58, ISSUE 2, P284-294, APRIL 24, 2008 0.1016/j.neuron.2008.03.020

---

[25] Olds J., Milner P. (1954). Positive reinforcement produced by electrical stimulation of the septal area and other regions of rat brain. J. Comp. Physiol. Psychol. 47, 419

[26] Berridge K. C. (2007). The debate over dopamine's role in reward: the case for incentive salience. *Psychopharmacology, 191*(3), 391–431. https://doi.org/10.1007/s00213-006-0578-x https://pubmed.ncbi.nlm.nih.gov/17072591/

[27] Olds J., Milner P. (1954). Positive reinforcement produced by electrical stimulation of the septal area and other regions of rat brain. J. Comp. Physiol. Psychol. 47, 419

[28] Sung (2013) Neuroscientific model of motivational process https://www.frontiersin.org/articles/10.3389/fpsyg.2013.00098/full

[29] Bayer and Glimcher (2005) *Midbrain Dopamine Neurones Encode a Quantitative Reward Prediction Error Signal* (2005) Neuron Vol 47, issue 1, 7 July 2005 pages 129-141

[30] Schultz, W., Carelli, R. M., & Wightman, R. M. (2015). Phasic dopamine signals: from subjective reward value to formal economic utility. *Current opinion in behavioral sciences, 5*, 147–154. https://doi.org/10.1016/j.cobeha.2015.09.006 https://www.ncbi.nlm.nih.gov/pmc/articles/PMC4692271/

[31] In fact, there is a big discussion in economics about the derivative concepts of cardinal and ordinal utility. Cardinal utility can be measured by the degree of perceived utility. However, ordinal utility cannot be measured as it is an assessment of relative preference. Yet by using careful statistical analysis with a standard preference scale (such as a 5-star Likert scale), you could start from an ordinal system to create a realistic cardinal system of absolute value as the volume of data grows.

[32] Stauffer, W. R., Lak, A., & Schultz, W. (2014). Dopamine reward prediction error responses reflect marginal utility. Current biology: CB, 24(21), 2491–2500. https://doi.org/10.1016/j.cub.2014.08.064

[33] Broome, J. (1991) *"Utility" Economics and Philosophy*, pages 1-12

---

[34] Investors in People (2019) https://www.investorsinpeople.com/wp-content/uploads/2019/06/Job-Exodus-2019-InvestorsInPeople.pdf

[35] Robbins Mike, *Harvard Business Review* Nov 2019. Why Employees Need Both Recognition and Appreciation.
https://hbr.org/2019/11/why-employees-need-both-recognition-and-appreciation

[36] Monito Adair, K. C., Rodriguez-Homs, L. G., Masoud, S., Mosca, P. J., & Sexton, J. B. (2020). Gratitude at Work: Prospective Cohort Study of a Web-Based, Single-Exposure Well-Being Intervention for Health Care Workers. Journal of medical Internet research, 22(5), e15562. https://doi.org/10.2196/15562
https://www.ncbi.nlm.nih.gov/pmc/articles/PMC7256751/

[37] Algoe, Sara B., and Jonathan Haidt.(2009) "Witnessing Excellence in Action: the 'Other-Praising' Emotions of Elevation, Gratitude, and Admiration." *The Journal of Positive Psychology*, vol. 4, no. 2, 2009, pp. 105–127., doi:10.1080/17439760802650519
https://www.ncbi.nlm.nih.gov/pmc/articles/PMC2689844/

[38] Positive Economy Institute (2019). *Positive Economy Index Nations.*
http://www.institut-economiepositive.com/wp-content/uploads/2019/03/INDICES_NATION-revue-ENG.pdf

[39] Gallup Q^{12} Research https://www.gallup.com/access/239210/gallup-q12-employee-engagement-survey.aspx

[40] Mosley Eric (2020) [30] Interview with Brené Brown
https://brenebrown.com/podcast/brene-with-eric-mosley-on-making-work-human/

[41] Robison J.,(2006). *In Praise of Praising Your Employees.* Gallup Business Journal, November 2006.
https://news.gallup.com/businessjournal/25369/praise-praising-your-employees.asp

42 Algoe, Sara B., and Jonathan Haidt.(2009) "Witnessing Excellence in Action: the 'Other-Praising' Emotions of Elevation, Gratitude, and Admiration." *The Journal of Positive Psychology*, vol. 4, no. 2, 2009, pp. 105–127., doi:10.1080/17439760802650519
https://www.ncbi.nlm.nih.gov/pmc/articles/PMC2689844/

43 Boston Consulting Group (2014). Global Talent Survey Report.
http://eskills2014conference.eu/fileadmin/conference2014/pdf/bcg%20dec oding%20global%20talent%20oct%202014.pdf

44 Algoe SB, Kurtz LE, Hilaire NM. Putting the "You" in "Thank You": Examining Other-Praising Behavior as the Active Relational Ingredient in Expressed Gratitude. *Social Psychological and Personality Science*. 2016;7(7):658-666. doi:10.1177/1948550616651681

45 Lawrence, Ma LK, Tunney RJ, Ferguson E. (2017) Does Gratitude Enhance Prosociality. A meta-analytical review; (Psychological Bulletin: http://www.apa.org/pubs/journals/bul/)

46 Algoe SB, Dwyer PC, Younge A, Oveis C. (2019), A new perspective on the social functions of emotions: Gratitude and the witnessing effect Journal of Personality and Social Psychology, 15 Aug 2019, 119(1):40-74DOI: 10.1037/pspi0000202 PMID: 31414873

47 American Psychological Association. (2016). APA survey finds feeling valued at work linked to well-being and performance.
https://www.apa.org/news/press/releases/2012/03/well-being

48 Monito Adair, K. C., Rodriguez-Homs, L. G., Masoud, S., Mosca, P. J., & Sexton, J. B. (2020). Gratitude at Work: Prospective Cohort Study of a Web-Based, Single-Exposure Well-Being Intervention for Health Care Workers. Journal of medical Internet research, 22(5), e15562. https://doi.org/10.2196/15562
https://www.ncbi.nlm.nih.gov/pmc/articles/PMC7256751/

49 American Psychological Association. (2016). APA survey finds feeling valued at work linked to well-being and performance.

[50] Harter, J and Adkins A. Are Your Star Employees Slipping Away? Gallup (2017). https://www.gallup.com/workplace/236351/star-employees-slipping-away.aspx

[51] Frith B, (2017) HR Magazine. Passion for work lost at age 42. http://hrmagazine.co.uk/article-details/passion-for-work-lost-at-age-42

[52] Lawrence, Ma LK, Tunney RJ, Ferguson E. (2017) Does Gratitude Enhance Prosociality. A meta-analytical review; (Psychological Bulletin: http://www.apa.org/pubs/journals/bul/)

[53] Morelli, S., Jared, T ,& Eisenberger, N. (2014) *Neural bases for feeling understood and not understood* Soc Cogn Affect Neurosci. 2014 Dec; 9(12): 1890–1896. Published online 2014 Feb 14. doi: PMCID: https://www.ncbi.nlm.nih.gov/pmc/articles/PMC4249470/ 24396002

[54] Boston Consulting Group (2014). Global Talent Survey Report. http://eskills2014conference.eu/fileadmin/conference2014/pdf/bcg%20decoding%20global%20talent%20oct%202014.pdf

[55] American Psychological Association. (2016). APA survey finds feeling valued at work linked to well-being and performance. https://www.apa.org/news/press/releases/2012/03/well-being

[56] Mankins, M. (2017), Great Companies should obsess over productivity not by efficiency, Harvard Business Review. https://hbr.org/2017/03/great-companies-obsess-over-productivity-not-efficiency

[57] Gallup (2020) *State of the Global Workplace Report.* https://www.gallup.com/workplace/238079/state-global-workplace-2017.aspx

[58] Nemo, J. (2014. *What a NASA janitor can teach us about living a bigger life.* https://www.bizjournals.com/bizjournals/how-to/growth-strategies/2014/12/what-a-nasa-janitor-can-teach-us.html

[59] Deloitte University Press (2017). *If you love them, set them free.*

[60] Beck, R.J and Harter, J. *Why Great Managers Are So Rare.*
https://www.gallup.com/workplace/231593/why-great-managers-rare.aspx
[61] Garner, R. *Half of UK graduates do not work in their field of study,
survey reveals.* https://www.independent.co.uk/student/news/half-uk-
graduates-do-not-work-their-field-study-survey-reveals-9574042.html
[62] Schwartz. B. (2005). The paradox of choice. TED Talk.
https://www.ted.com/talks/barry_schwartz_the_paradox_of_choice

[63] Cacha, Lleuvelyn & Poznanski, R. & Latif, Ahmad & Tengku,
Mohammad. (2019). Psychophysiology of Chronic Stress: An Example of
Mind-Body Interaction. NeuroQuantology. 17. 53-63.
10.14704/nq.2019.17.07.2562.
https://www.researchgate.net/publication/336920120_Psychophysiology_o
f_Chronic_Stress_An_Example_of_Mind-body_Interaction
[64] Gregory J. Quirk, Francisco Sotres-Bayon, Signalling Aversive Events in
the Midbrain: Worse than Expected,
Neuron, Volume 61, Issue 5, 2009, Pages 655-656, ISSN 0896-6273,
https://doi.org/10.1016/j.neuron.2009.02.016
[65] Cacha, Lleuvelyn & Poznanski, R. & Latif, Ahmad & Tengku,
Mohammad. (2019). Psychophysiology of Chronic Stress: An Example of
Mind-Body Interaction. NeuroQuantology. 17. 53-63.
10.14704/nq.2019.17.07.2562.
https://www.researchgate.net/publication/336920120_Psychophysiology_o
f_Chronic_Stress_An_Example_of_Mind-body_Interaction
[66] Greifeneder, R., Scheibehenne, B., & Kleber, N. (2010 Less may be more
when choosing is difficult: Choice complexity and too much choice. *Acta
Psychologica, 133*(1), 45-50.
[67] Udemy (2016) Workplace Boredom Report.
https://research.udemy.com/research_report/2016-workplace-boredom-
report/
[68] Perkbox. *The Financial Cost of Employee Disengagement.*
https://www.perkbox.com/uk/resources/library/interactive-the-financial-
cost-of-employee-disengagement

[69] van Hooft, E., & van Hooff, M. (2018). The state of boredom: Frustrating or depressing? *Motivation and emotion, 42*(6), 931–946. (https://doi.org/10.1007/s11031-018-9710-6

[70] Cohen JY, Haesler S, Vong L, Lowell BB, Uchida N. Neuron-type-specific signals for reward and punishment in the ventral tegmental area. *Nature.* 2012;482(7383):85-88. Published 2012 Jan 18. doi:10.1038/nature10754
https://www.ncbi.nlm.nih.gov/pmc/articles/PMC3271183/

[71] Likert, Rensis *A technique for the measurement of attitudes.* Archives of psychology (1932). p. 7

[72] BitDegree (2021). *Ripple vs Bitcoin: What's the Better Alternative?*
https://www.bitdegree.org/crypto/tutorials/ripple-vs-bitcoin

[73] Biro, M. (2013) *5 Ways Leaders rock Employee Recognition.* Forbes.
https://www.forbes.com/sites/meghanbiro/2013/01/13/5-ways-leaders-rock-employee-recognition/?sh=3af649cc47ca

[74] Slaughter, R. (2014). *10 Best Practices for Enhanced Employee Engagement.* AccelaWork Business Development.
https://www.accelawork.com/infographic-10-best-practices-for-enhanced-employee-engagement/

[75] Gallup Q^{12} Research https://www.gallup.com/access/239210/gallup-q12-employee-engagement-survey.aspx

[76] CultureAmp Employee Engagement Software.
https://www.cultureamp.com/products/employee-engagement-2/

[77] Hanushek, E. (2011). Economic Value of Higher Teacher Quality-Economics of Education Review 30 2011 p. 466-479.

[78] Hanushek, E. (2011) Valuing Teachers: How Much is a Good Teacher Worth? http://hanushek.stanford.edu/publications/valuing-teachers-how-much-good-teacher-worth